IMAGES
of America

NEW MEXICO STATE POLICE

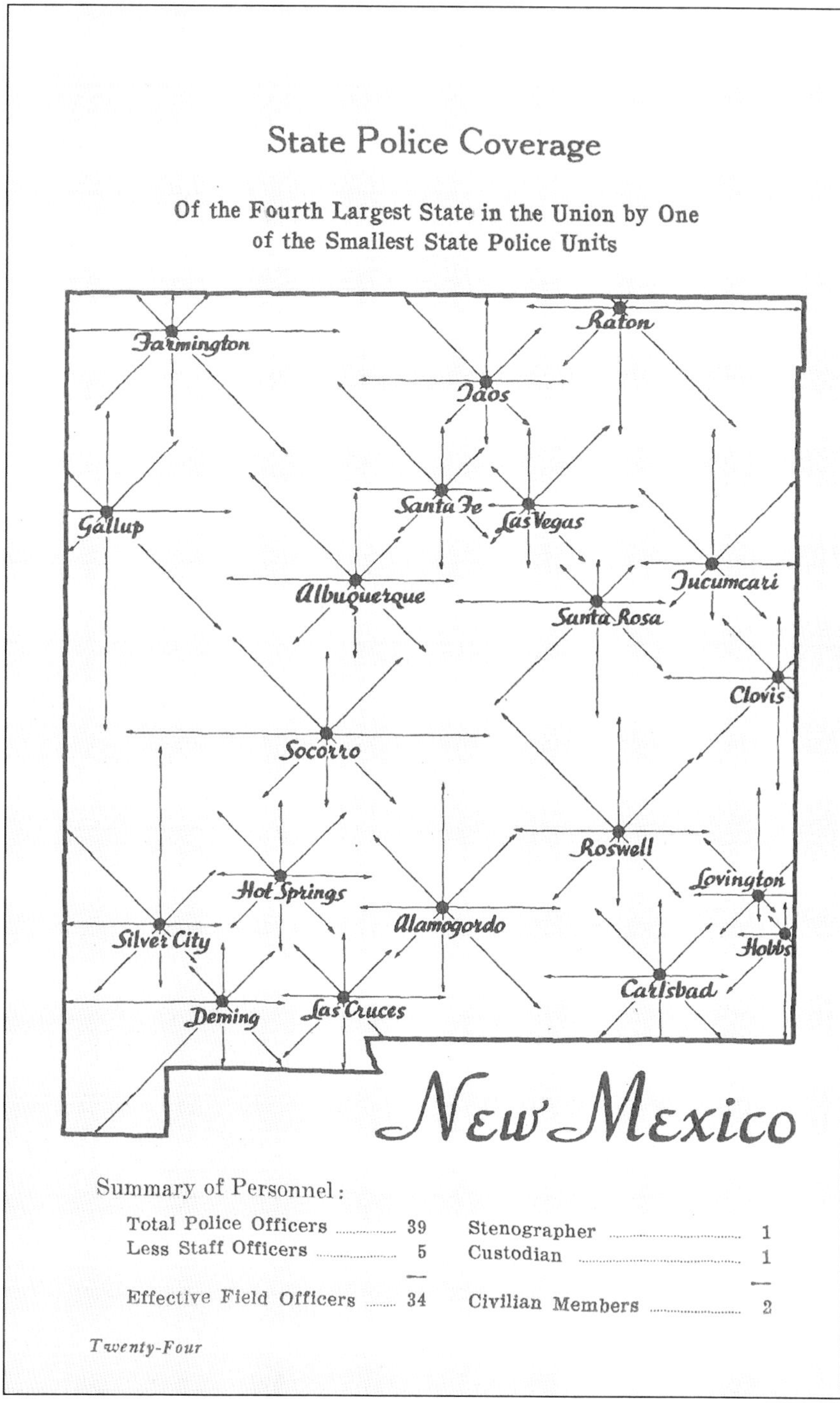

State Police Coverage

Of the Fourth Largest State in the Union by One of the Smallest State Police Units

Summary of Personnel:

Total Police Officers	39	Stenographer	1
Less Staff Officers	5	Custodian	1
Effective Field Officers	34	Civilian Members	2

Twenty-Four

This map shows the New Mexico State Police districts in 1939 and the manpower of the department that covered those districts. (Courtesy of the author.)

On the Cover: Members of the New Mexico State Police pose in Albuquerque for a publicity photograph in 1939. (Courtesy of New Mexico State Tourist Bureau.)

IMAGES
of America

NEW MEXICO STATE POLICE

Ronald Taylor

ARCADIA
PUBLISHING

ISBN 978-1-4671-2999-2

Published by Arcadia Publishing
Charleston, South Carolina

Printed in the United States of America

Library of Congress Control Number: 2013937110

For all general information, please contact Arcadia Publishing:
Telephone 843-853-2070
Fax 843-853-0044
E-mail sales@arcadiapublishing.com
For customer service and orders:
Toll-Free 1-888-313-2665

Visit us on the Internet at www.arcadiapublishing.com

This book is dedicated to a friend of all law enforcement, Michael Trompak of Timeless Images in Albuquerque, New Mexico. Mike passed away on September 20, 2012.

Contents

ACKNOWLEDGMENTS

First, I would like to thank my wife, Sherrie, for all of her support and for letting me fill up our garage with my collections. Every time I came back from State Police Headquarters with boxes of papers, she would just shake her head.

Many people have helped in my history collecting. There are too many to name here, but I want to thank retired state police chief John Denko. I also want to thank retired chief and Department of Public Safety cabinet secretary Richard C de Baca and Al Regensberg from the New Mexico State Archives.

I could never have done any of the research if not for Theresa Royal, who would go to the state archives and pick up boxes of files for me to go through.

Chuck Hornung, the author of several books on the New Mexico Mounted Police, inspired my writing and collecting. I offer thanks for his advice.

Fellow historian and State Police Agent Norman Rhoades would help me collect photographs and help interview families of the "old-timers." He is the one person I could throw ideas back and forth with. My thanks go to all the state police personnel, commissioned and civilian, who kept their eyes open for artifacts and historical paperwork stashed somewhere and who would give them to me.

I want to thank all of the families of the early motor patrol and state police officers that shared their time and photographs with me. I especially thank retired state police captain Floyd Miles and retired state police chief Kenneth K. Miller, who provided me with lots of information and photographs. A special thanks goes to Jack House, whose father, E.J. House, was chief of the motor patrol and the first chief of the state police. Jack shared memories and his father's scrapbooks and memorabilia with me.

Mike Trompak of Timeless Images copied many photographs and helped with my collection. Thanks go to Joann Martinez Luera, Mike's "work wife," for putting up with us and for her help.

All images are from my personal collection unless otherwise noted.

INTRODUCTION

Over the centuries, men and women from many nationalities have discovered the enchanting natural beauty that is New Mexico. During its first 60 years under American rule, the land earned the nickname the Sunshine Territory; upon being granted statehood in 1912, the 47th member of the federal union became the Turquoise State. Today, New Mexico is known around the world as the Land of Enchantment. But to understand the state's captivating aura, a person must first appreciate not only the land, but its people.

New Mexico has always been a land of magnificent scenery. It covers 121,666 square miles of mountains and deserts, equal to the combined area of the New England states, and includes 78 million acres of timber, water, livestock range, and farmland. The Enchanted Land has never been a melting pot of culture or racial heritage. The native Indians, the Spanish or Mexicans, Nuevomexicanos, Anglos, and other ethnic groups have each clung to their social and political relationships. The Land of Enchantment is a cultural mosaic; its wealth is in its multicultural composition. This mix kept New Mexico a territory of the United States for over six decades, and it was the conflicts of becoming an American people that finally led the 1905 New Mexico Territorial Legislative Assembly to authorize the creation of a territorial police force.

In the early 20th century, members of the Ranger Service of Texas effectively killed or chased undesirable citizens residing in the western section of their state even further west across the plains. Meanwhile, the Arizona Rangers, established in 1901 to bring law and order to the Silver Territory, forced badmen eastward over the border mountains and into the New Mexico Territory. Receiving the results of this joint law enforcement effort quickly made New Mexico the final catch basin for the flotsam and jetsam of frontier humanity.

New Mexicans have always been an independent people devoted to family and community, but most citizens recognize the need for a set of guidelines that set the parameters of civilized conduct. The Native Americans who first settled the Land of Enchantment set up a mutually acceptable society for their lives. They reached a working relationship with the Spanish and, later, Mexican settlers that came to their homeland. Decades later, another people with a different language and culture arrived in Santa Fe. In 1878, with the advent of the railroad, settlers came west by the thousands and brought with them a new social framework and legal system. The suddenness with which things happened during the last half of the 19th century in the New Mexico Territory, the land of the unexpected, made any code for human behavior more or less a mockery. In 1890, the federal government declared that the frontier era of the Wild West was history, but the general impression, in New Mexico, was that crime knew no limit and that the gun was still the final answer to all problems.

The territory's leaders understood that New Mexico's progress, its self-government under statehood, hinged upon citizen safety and business security maintained by a central police authority. It was a lifetime ago, in the waning days of the frontier during civil crisis, that New Mexico's Rangers, the mounted police, was hammered to life, and for 15 years the men did their jobs. Fred

Lambert, the last living member of the territorial police, summed it up this way: "It was a tough job that needed doing and we boys just done it. Nothing more; nothing less. We got paid to do a job and we done it." Those words sum up the heritage of the New Mexico Mounted Police.

Winds from the distant past have blown away the smell of gunpowder, but those hard days survive as glorified legends. The Rangers had been dead for a decade before New Mexico's leaders again felt the need for a statewide police presence in the "modern era." During the Depression gangster era, in 1933, the state legislature authorized creating a 10-man motorcycle unit to patrol the state's highway system and render aid to travelers. This unit was the New Mexico Motor Patrol. Two years later, these men became the foundation of the present-day state police.

The new force was designed to continue the duties of the motor patrol, but with expanded police authority and a mandate to assist local officers in restoring and maintaining law and order in a state overrun with bootleggers and illegal gambling operations. The state police adopted the motto *Pro Bono Publico* (For the Public Good) and started a long-running tradition of public service. For three quarters of a century, the men and women of the New Mexico State Police have worn the black-and-gray uniform and displayed the gold shield of their ancestors.

These 21st-century officers seldom ride horses, but drive high-powered patrol cars and fly high-tech aircraft. There are special units within the force trained in crime scene investigation, bomb handling, emergency response, and tactical weapons, and undercover special agents infiltrate crime gangs. The governor has an executive protection detail skilled in public safety. In short, as the New Mexico State Police, now a division of the state's department of public safety, moves through the last quarter of its first century of operation, it is prepared to combat modern high-tech criminals seeking to do business in the Land of Enchantment.

Over a quarter of a century has passed since I first met Ronald Taylor. I was deep into researching my histories of the New Mexico Mounted Police, predecessor of the state police, and he was an active officer of the New Mexico State Police. Sergeant Taylor contacted me for permission to use some of my photographs and mounted police information in a state police yearbook he was editing. Over the years, we shared an interest in preserving primary history of the struggle to establish centralized law enforcement in New Mexico. During the years that Ron Taylor served as editor of the New Mexico State Police Association's magazine, the *Roadrunner*, he faced one of his biggest challenges by tracking down information on the officers from the early years of his beloved state police. This book is possible because he was able to persuade the old-timers or their family members to share their memories and photographs.

The collection of historic uniforms, police equipment, and photographs that Taylor helped to compile are the central focus of the state police history display that lines both sides of the entry hallway leading from the security checkpoint into the headquarters complex in Santa Fe. Taylor is the unofficial historian for the New Mexico State Police.

Saddle up and hold on tight, because you have a great ride ahead. It is time to explore the history of the New Mexico State Police, one of the oldest such organizations in the nation.

—Chuck Hornung
Author of *New Mexico's Rangers: The Mounted Police*

One

The New Mexico Motor Patrol

From 1921, when the New Mexico Mounted Police ceased to exist, until the 1930s, there was no state law enforcement in New Mexico. As the years went on, there was an increase in automobile and truck traffic. By the end of 1932, the highway system in the state consisted of 358,210 miles of maintained roads.

There were no speed laws for cars on the state's highways. Motorists were expected to operate passenger automobiles at such speeds as were consistent with safety and proper use of the roads. Trucks and buses were limited to a maximum speed of 45 miles per hour.

Numerous laws were in the books for vehicle lighting, but no operator's license was required. The minimum age for an operator was 14.

Enforcement of these laws could easily be achieved in townships and within city limits, but on the open roads and highways they could not be enforced, because there was no highway patrol like in the neighboring states.

The state of New Mexico had several field men from various state agencies who enforced laws pertaining to motor vehicles. The highway department was interested in seeing that all of the laws were equally enforced, because most of the revenue from all branches of government went eventually to the construction and maintenance of roads.

With the various sets of field men scattered over the state, it was inevitable that duplication and the overlapping of duties would occur. It became apparent to the state government that a single group of men, under a central control, would be optimal. This new agency would be called the New Mexico Motor Patrol.

In February 1933, with the backing of Gov. Arthur Seligman, Senate Bill 105 passed, forming the motor patrol. For the positions of chief and nine patrolmen, 231 applications were received. Of the 30 men who passed the written test, 19 were assigned to the 30-day school and 10 were hired after their completion of the academy.

Gov. Arthur Seligman. Governor Seligman was instrumental in the creation of the New Mexico Motor Patrol. He supported the introduction of Senate Bill 105 in the 1933 legislative session. He died in office on September 24, 1933. (Courtesy of Adrian Diamond-Box.)

Frank Horn. Frank Horn, a supervisor with the tour group Indian Detours, was assigned to oversee the technical aspects of the motor patrol school. He is in the first row, at center. His daughter, Jeanne, is also in the photograph. In the back row, third from the left, is one of the tour guides, future motor patrolman Lacy Shortridge. (Courtesy of Jeanne Thorwaldsen.)

APPLICANT PHOTOGRAPH. Applicants for the New Mexico Motor Patrol were required to submit a photograph of themselves with no shirt. Carlos Salas was one of the original motor patrolmen and the only one to finish his career with the New Mexico State Police. He retired on September 30, 1959.

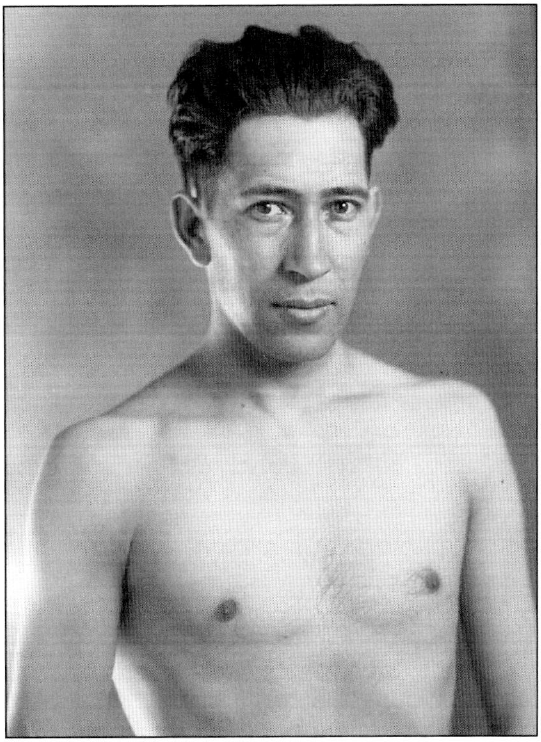

CAPT. HOMER GARRISON. Captain Garrison was a member of the Texas Highway Patrol. The New Mexico Motor Patrol was going to pattern itself after the Texas version. Chief L.G. Phares of the highway patrol was asked to loan one of his officers to run the motor patrol school. Captain Garrison was given a leave of absence to train the New Mexico officers.

New Motorcycles. On July 30, 1933, ten 1934 Harley-Davidson motorcycles were delivered to the motor patrol at St. Michael's School in Santa Fe. The men pictured are motor patrol chief Earl Irish (left), Homer Garrison (center), and Albuquerque Harley-Davidson dealer Kenneth Miller. In 1937, Miller joined the state police and rose to the rank of chief of the department.

Chief Earl Irish. On July 27, 1933, recruit Irish was appointed the first chief of the motor patrol. When the patrol became the state police in 1935, Irish became a state policeman and was one of the first sergeants of the department in 1936. (Courtesy of Bob Irish.)

Graduation Day. The new motor patrolmen graduated on August 2, 1933. Here, the men are lined up to receive their badges at St. Michael's High School. On the left is Attorney General Ernest K. Neumann. The patrolmen wore forest green uniforms with tan shirts. The boots and Sam Browne belts were made of brown leather.

The Badge of Office. The New Mexico Motor Patrol badge was made of polished brass. The seal on the badge has the Roman numerals MDCCCLV (1855), which was the date New Mexico became a territory. It is not known why the territorial seal on the badge was used instead of the state seal, since New Mexico became a state in 1912.

Motor Patrol Shoulder Patch. The patch was worn on the left shoulder of the winter shirt and dress blouse. Some officers wore it on the summer shirt as well. The words and wheel were made of yellow thread and the background was forest green. The winged wheel logo was worn by traffic officers throughout the United States.

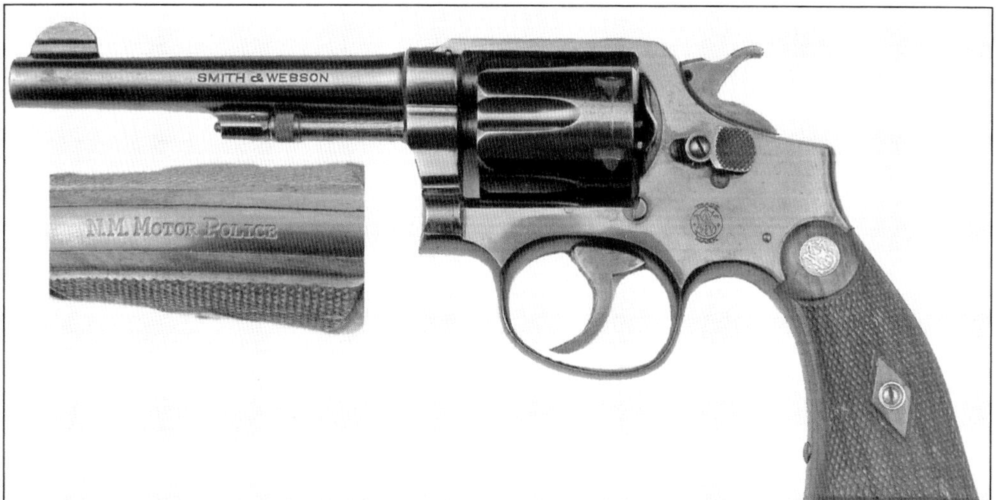

Motor Patrol Weapon. The New Mexico Motor Patrol Board of Supervisors ordered 12 revolvers from Smith & Wesson. The chosen weapon was the .38 Hand Ejector, Military and Police Model. This is the only handgun in motor patrol or state police history that had the name of the organization stamped on it. (Courtesy of Jack House.)

New Mexico Capitol. The motor patrol headquarters office was in the basement in the rear of the building. Working in the office were the chief, one patrolman, and a part-time clerk. (Courtesy of Museum of New Mexico, photograph by Christian G. Kaadt, Neg. No. 10392.)

First Day at Work. On August 5, 1933, the patrolmen are lined up in front of the state capitol building on their first day of work before going to their duty stations. Shown here are, from left to right, Chief Earl Irish, Patrolmen Phillip Coyle, Ivan Johnson, Lacy Shortridge, and Carlos Salas, Gov. Arthur Seligman, Patrolmen Henry Eager, M.G. Benavides, E.J. House, Charles Miller, and I.G. Beckner.

New Mexico Motor Patrol Bulletin

OFFICIAL PUBLICATION OF NEW MEXICO SHERIFFS AND PEACE OFFICERS

FOR THE INFORMATION OF COMMISSIONED EMPLOYES ONLY

New Mexico Motor Patrol broadcasts over Station KOB daily except Sunday

VOL. 1 No. 21 SANTA FE, NEW MEXICO, MAY 15, 1934. CHIEF'S OFFICE

N. M. M. PATROL

BOARD OF SUPERVISORS

GOV. A. W. HOCKENHULL

ATT. GEN. E. K. NEUMANN—Chairman

HY. ENG. C. D. MACY—Secretary

E. J. HOUSE, JR.—Chief

PATROLMEN

EARL IRISH—No. 1

WILLIAM KATZ—No. 2

PHILLIP E. COYLE—No. 3

GILBERT BECKNER—No. 4

CHAS. H. MILLER—No. 5

IVAN L. JOHNSON—No. 6

LACY A. SHORTRIDGE—No. 7

CARLOS C. SALAS—No. 8

HENRY EAGER—No. 9

F. J. HORN—Special Deputy

J. A. BLACK—Special Deputy

DISTRICT STATIONS

ALBUQUERQUE, N. M.

ROSWELL, N. M.

RATON, N. M.

LAS CRUCES, N. M.

HEADQUARTERS, SANTA FE.

STOLEN FROM NATIONAL GUARD WAREHOUSE AT CHEYENNE, WYOMING

One 30 caliber Browning automatic rifle, No. 100726.

One 30 caliber Browning automatic rifle, No. 250237.

One 22 caliber Springfield bolt action rifle, No. 977.

One-half case of Winchester 22 caliber ammunition. 500 rounds.

Two Underwood standard typewriters, numbers 1075482 and 1067934.

One brass telescope, make unknown.

One pair Army shoes, size 7½.

If any of these articles are found on any person, hold and notify Sheriff Geo. J. Carrol at Cheyenne, Wyoming, or New Mexico Motor Patrol.

LOST OR STOLEN LICENSE PLATES

N. M. passenger No. 51-890.

N. M. passenger No. 9700.

PICKUPS

Arrest E. B. Williams, age 35 years, weight 145 pounds, height 5 feet 9 inches, dark complexion, and wears glasses. Driving a gray Plymouth convertible coupe, Illinois license No. 441-110. Motor No. PA50042, serial No. 1615800. Top has been patched. Has 4 Pharis Grip tires. Goodyear spare and red wire wheels. Seat covers badly worn. Hold car and occupants and notify New Mexico Motor Patrol.

Ford V-8 coach, color tan, Wyoming license No. 2-5880, motor No. 18-761-503. Car and occupants wanted by sheriff at Cheyenne, Wyoming, for removing mortgaged property.

1934 Plymouth De Luxe sedan, black body and fenders, gold stripe. Steel wheels. Goodyear tires, metal tire cover. 2 Dual horns, tail lights and windshield wipers. Motor No. PE 25 538, serial No. 2 210 284, Colorado dealer's license No. 1-D668. Hold car and occupants for this office.

1932 Plymouth coach, black color. Equipped with wire wheels, metal tire cover. Pan below front of radiator dented. Metropolitan agent's brief case in car when stolen. Motor No. PC-104274, serial No. 1844150, Kansas license No. 47-1248.

1929 Ford sport coupe, green body with yellow stripe, black fenders, black wire wheels. Motormeter, front tires Goodyear, rear tires Riverside. New Sport top, right front fender welded, right door upholstery torn near the pocket. Stolen in Denver, Colo.

1931 De Soto sedan, blue body with black wheels and fenders. One fender well on left side. Motor No. SA-1883, serial No. 5012128, Minnesota license No. B- 13386. Stolen car.

1930 Essex roadster, yellow body, black top and had six wire wheels. Motor No. 1246065, serial No. 1169858, Minnesota license No. B-104438. Stolen car.

1934 Pontiac sedan, black color, has small hole in windshield, equipped with radio. Motor No. 984305, serial No. 846952, body No. P4129, New Mexico license No. 42826. Stolen May 12, 1934.

No. 1. A. N. Israel, age 45 years, weight 120 pounds, height 5 feet 5 inches, dried up face.

No. 2. F. M. Woods, age 28 years, height 6 feet, weight 185 pounds, reddish complexon.

When last seen they were traveling in two cars—a model T Ford pickup

LATEST INFORMATION ON CLYDE BARROWS

Has been operating in west and northwest Texas and he may try to contact relatives in Carlsbad, N. M. It is believed that Barrow is traveling with Bonnie Parker, a party by the name of Methvin and another party by the name of Palmer. Barrow, Methvin and Palmer have recently been seen wearing soft blue hats and dark goggles. Traveling in a Ford V-8 sedan or a Pontiac sedan. Bonnie Parker keeps a white rabbit with her all of the time.

ORDERS TO PATROLMEN

When on Patrol Duty on the highways either in cars or motorcycles, you are not to pick up any person or persons to give them a lift, unless it is a case of necessity.

Keep a close check on Highway equipment and Highway gates. In many cases highway gates have been taken down and strands of wire put in their places. Place under arrest any persons having these gates in their possession who are not authorized to have same.

CHECK ARTIST

F. G. Wilson, American. Age 35 years, height 5 feet 9 or 10 inches, weight 150 pounds, small mustache, wearing light grey suit, tan shoes and light grey hat, turned down in front.

Last check this man passed was on the Denver National Bank of Denver, Colo. Check was typewritten and a check protector was used.

This man gives check for about twice as much as the purchase, receiving the balance in cash. He then tells merchant that his wife will call for the purchase.

Forward any information to Sheriff Geo. J. Carroll, at Cheyenne, Wyoming, or New Mexico Motor Patrol.

COURTESY CALL

Arno Prueggaman, age 40 years, height 6 feet, light complexion, blue eyes, blond hair, slightly bald, mustache.

This man left the De Vargas hotel at Santa Fe, N. M., May 9, 1934, where he left his baggage and belongings. Wanted badly by his wife in Raton, N. M. If located, do not hold, but notify him that his wife is ill, or notify New Mexico Motor Patrol.

MOTOR PATROL BULLETIN. On December 19, 1933, Chief House started a weekly bulletin that he mailed to all law enforcement agencies in New Mexico and surrounding states. The bulletins listed stolen cars and merchandise and wanted subjects. All law enforcement agencies were encouraged to submit information. This particular bulletin, dated May 15, 1934, lists information on Clyde Barrow and Bonnie Parker. (Courtesy of Jack House.)

TRUCK ACCIDENT. Motor Patrolman E.J. House investigates an overturned truck in September 1933 outside of Santa Fe, New Mexico.

On Patrol. In August 1933, Motor Patrolmen Ivan Johnson (left) and Phillip Coyle are on duty on their motorcycles in Deming, New Mexico. (Courtesy of Mary Carter and Helen Philips.)

Publicity Photograph. Chief Earl Irish (left) and Patrolmen E.J. House (center) and Charles Miller are on patrol outside of Santa Fe, New Mexico, in September 1933. The motorcycles are equipped with one clear spotlight and one red spotlight. Chief Irish wears a gold band on his hat to designate his rank. (Courtesy of Jack House.)

Traffic Stop. Patrolman E.J. House makes a traffic stop on a highway department car while Patrolman Charles Miller waits on his motorcycle. In September 1933, the State of New Mexico started cracking down on the unauthorized use of state vehicles. (Courtesy of Jack House.)

Chief Ely J. House. E.J. House was appointed the chief of the motor patrol on October 5, 1933. When Governor Seligman died, Lt. Gov. A.W. Hockenhull assumed the office. He appointed House because of his prior police experience. In this photograph, Chief House is wearing the winter uniform. (Courtesy of Jack House.)

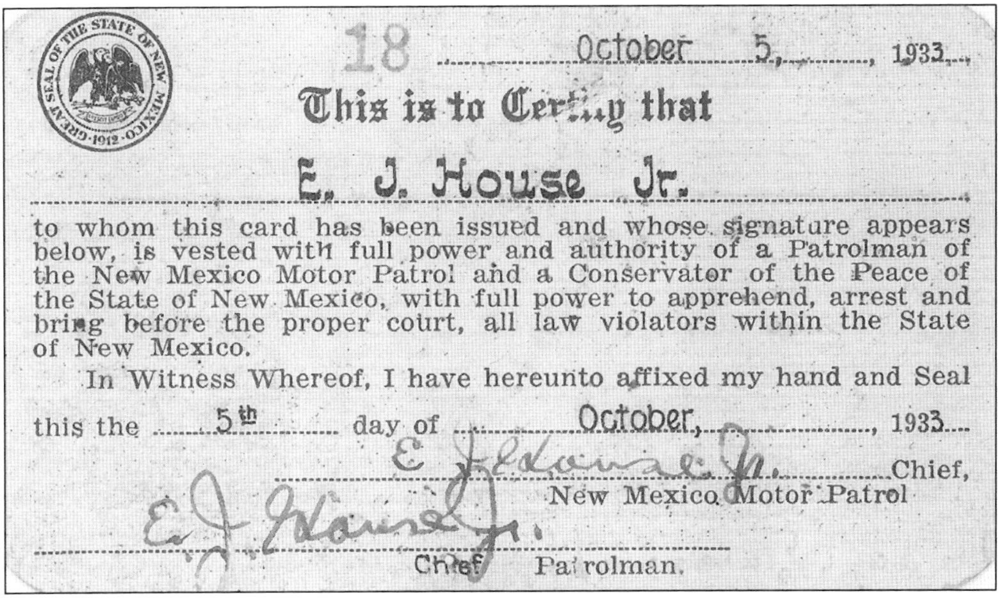
18 October 5, 1933

This is to Certify that

E. J. House Jr.

to whom this card has been issued and whose signature appears below, is vested with full power and authority of a Patrolman of the New Mexico Motor Patrol and a Conservator of the Peace of the State of New Mexico, with full power to apprehend, arrest and bring before the proper court, all law violators within the State of New Mexico.

In Witness Whereof, I have hereunto affixed my hand and Seal this the 5th day of October, 1933

E J House Jr. Chief,
New Mexico Motor Patrol

E J House Jr.
Chief Patrolman.

Commission Card. This is a commission card issued to Chief House. Every patrolman carried a card such as this to prove that he was a motor patrolman. Commission cards are used to this day by law enforcement officers. (Courtesy of Jack House.)

Patrolman Carlos Salas. Patrolman Salas was stationed in Roswell in 1933. The motor patrol had changed the boots and Sam Browne belt from brown to black leather. Salas is wearing the summer uniform and an unauthorized long tie. Motor officers throughout the United States wore bow ties because they would not blow in the wind. (Courtesy of Doe Sales.)

Patrolman Marin G. Benavides. Patrolman Benavides was stationed in Raton after completing recruit school. He had to leave the patrol after two months because riding motorcycles on unpaved roads aggravated an old illness. A World War I veteran, Benavides was close to 50 years old at the time of this photograph. (Courtesy of Josephine Bonham.)

Patrolman Henry Eager. Patrolman Eager was stationed in Roswell with Carlos Salas. He left the patrol in November 1934 and later served time as a state senator. This photograph was taken in the Sacramento Mountains between Roswell and Alamogordo. (Courtesy of Murph Eager.)

In-Service School. On July 16, 1934, the motor patrol held an in-service school at St. Michael's to train current and replacement patrolmen. Lined up here are, from left to right, Patrolmen Ivan Johnson, Lacy Shortridge, Henry Eager, and Charles Miller, board of supervisors attorney general E.K. Neumann, Gov. A.H. Hockenhull, state highway engineer Glenn Macy, Chief E.J. House, and Patrolmen Roy Vermillion, Gilbert Beckner, Carlos Salas, and Earl Irish.

Patrolman Charles Miller. Patrolman Miller was stationed in Raton after recruit school. On July 16, 1934, he was promoted to assistant chief. Miller left the patrol on January 15, 1935. In this photograph, Miller is wearing a .45 Colt automatic. Note the holster on the front fork of the motorcycle. There is another .45 pistol in that holster, with a shoulder stock attached. (Courtesy of Jack House.)

PATROLMAN IVAN GILBERT BECKNER. Patrolman Beckner was first stationed in Albuquerque. During his motor patrol career, he also served in Raton, Clovis, and Roswell. Beckner was one of the patrolmen who transitioned over to the New Mexico State Police. He left the department on December 14, 1936. He was the last surviving original motor patrolman when he passed away on December 3, 1994. (Courtesy of Stan Beckner and Nancy Watt.)

ROADBLOCK IN LORDSBURG. Members of the motor patrol are conducting a traffic safety check with deputies of the Hidalgo County Sheriff's Department. This photograph, from around April 1935, was taken after the patrol was made into the New Mexico State Police. Pictured here in uniform are, from left to right, Patrolmen Jack Dean, Fidel Gonzales, and Ivan Johnson. The other men are unidentified. (Courtesy of Mary Carter and Helen Philips.)

Two

The Beginning of 75 Years of Service and the Depression Era

It had been a year and a half since the beginning of the New Mexico Motor Patrol. Due to the increase in motor vehicle traffic and calls for service, there was a need to expand the patrol from the current 10 patrolmen.

Through the untiring efforts of Chief House, and with the full support of Gov. Clyde Tingley, a bill was introduced in the 12th state legislature to create the New Mexico State Police. House Bill 30 passed the legislature and became law on February 25, 1935, with an emergency clause. On that day, the New Mexico Motor Patrol ceased to exist and the New Mexico State Police came into existence, with all motor patrolmen automatically becoming state policemen. By law, the force was to consist of a chief and not more than 30 policemen, including wearers of derbies and broad-toe shoes, otherwise known as plainclothesmen. The law provided for a captain, a lieutenant, and no more than three sergeants.

On April 6, 1935, the first New Mexico State Police School started, with 30 prospective policemen vying to fill slots for 15 additional officers. By the end of the school session, 27 recruits remained. In the end, fifteen men were put to work and four were put on reserve. The initial class graduated on May 29, 1935. Two detectives and one desk sergeant were hired without attending the police school. The school was conducted at the National Guard Armory in Santa Fe, New Mexico.

With the decision to put the officers in cars instead of motorcycles, seven 1935 Chevrolet police cars were purchased and equipped with red and white spotlights. The number of districts was expanded to 12, with two men assigned to each district. The work schedule consisted of 12-hour days, with one day off every two weeks.

The new uniform consisted of black oxford gray breeches and hat, along with a gray shirt. In 1938, Chief House designed the new dress blouse using his son Jack's crayons.

GOV. CLYDE TINGLEY. Clyde Tingley was elected governor of New Mexico and took office on January 1, 1935, serving two terms until January 1, 1939. Governor Tingley was a very strong supporter of the New Mexico State Police.

CHIEF E.J. HOUSE. House was the first chief of the New Mexico State Police. He left the department after Gov. John Miles took office on January 1, 1939. (Courtesy of Jack House.)

Colt New Service Revolver. In 1935, the state police purchased the .45 Colt New Service Revolvers with the five-and-one-half-inch barrel for its officers. Seen here is a set of pearl grips that a patrolman attached to the pistol.

State Police Badge. A new badge was designed and chosen for the New Mexico State Police to replace the motor patrol badge. It was made by L.A. Stamp Company in California. The same style of badge is worn by the state police to this day.

SHOULDER PATCH. A shoulder patch was designed for the new organization. The wording was produced with black thread, and the first patch had yellow thread for a background. The background was soon changed to gray for several years and then changed to white in the late 1930s. The white patch is still being used by the state police today. (Courtesy of Agent Norman Rhoades.)

PATROL CAR. The state police decided to outfit the patrolmen with cars. The department kept 10 older motorcycles and purchased seven Chevrolet cars for $610 each. The car was equipped with a white spotlight and a red spotlight. Two officers were assigned to ride in each car. (Courtesy of Hal Kerr.)

Officers with Their Unit. Patrolmen Charlie Eagleton and Hal Kerr stand next to their patrol car in 1935. Both patrolmen were stationed in Vaughn, New Mexico. The hats sported silver cords, but this initial feature was later replaced with a band. (Courtesy of Hal Kerr.)

Carlsbad Caverns National Park. These patrolmen pose in Carlsbad Caverns during an event in 1935. Shown here are Penn Winston (left), Jack Nichols (center), and Curt Lawhon.

NEW STATE POLICE OFFICE. A new, bigger state police office was needed for the expanded force. With the help of the Works Progress Administration, this office was built on Cerrillos Road, in Santa Fe. The state police moved into the office on November 8, 1935. Standing in the front is Sgt. Harrie Dalbey. (Courtesy of the State Records Center & Archives, DOD Collection.)

NEW OFFICE DEDICATION. On December 18, 1935, Governor Tingley raised the US flag in front of the new headquarters. At a dedication ceremony on that day, the state police announced the promotions of a captain, a lieutenant, and three sergeants. These were the first supervisor promotions for the new state police. (Courtesy of Jack House.)

Night Shift at Headquarters. Patrolmen stationed in Santa Fe during 1935 took turns working the desk at headquarters during the night. Shown here in the office are Patrolmen Gilbert Beckner (left), Walter Darr (center), and Jimmie Elliot.

Dona Ana County Floods. In September 1935, the Southern New Mexico county of Dona Ana flooded when the Rio Grande River overflowed its banks. Patrolman Al Hathaway is seen checking the depth of the river.

Fatal Accident. One of a patrolman's duties was to investigate traffic accidents. Here, Patrolmen Hal Kerr and John Wootten investigate an accident on the construction road to Conchas Dam on January 10, 1936.

New Supervisor. Effective January 1, 1936, new promotions took effect. On the left is one of the three new sergeants, Earl Irish. Also seen here is Bennie Duran, who lost his leg in a motorcycle accident in 1937. Since the state had no disability retirement, he stayed with the department, working in the headquarters until he passed away in 1963.

Southern Patrolmen. These are the patrolmen stationed in Lordsburg, Deming, and Las Cruces in 1936. Shown are, from left to right, Fidel Gonzales, Issie Funk, Ivan Johnson, and Al Hathaway.

Motorist Assistance. Patrolmen Issie Funk (left) and Penn Winston are seen assisting a stranded motorist in 1936.

Missing Prohibition Agent. On August 28, 1930, Prohibition agent Ray Sutton disappeared in Northern New Mexico while working a case on bootlegging. His body was never found. On April 2, 1936, information was received that Agent Sutton's body could be found in a water-filled hole called the Devil's Wash Basin in Northern New Mexico. State police drained the lake and for several days searched the area with no results.

Missing Tourists. On May 22, 1935, four tourists from Illinois disappeared while passing through New Mexico. An investigation involving the FBI and state police was initiated, but nothing was ever found of the tourists. In June 1936, information was received that the bodies were in the Bottomless Lakes near Roswell. A search by a diver was undertaken, but no bodies were found. The case is still unsolved.

Marijuana Seizure. On August 12, 1936, the state police, along with the Mora County sheriff's office, seized 6,000 marijuana plants at Ocate. Pictured here with some of the plants are Patrolman A.B. Martinez (left), an unidentified sheriff of Mora County, and Capt. Roy Vermillion (right).

Sgt. Harrie Dalbey. Sergeant Dalbey, a retired US Army captain and a World War I veteran, was hired in April 1935 to run the office for the state police. Dalbey was the only member of the department authorized to wear slacks instead of breeches. Here, he is at his desk in 1938 wearing the new uniform shirt that replaced the gray shirt in 1936.

New Motorcycles. To increase visibility, the state police decided to put their men on motorcycles once more. In April 1937, thirty-two Harley-Davidson motorcycles were delivered to the state police. On the day that the motorcycles were delivered, Patrolmen Penn Winston (left) and Bill Ehret pose for a photograph.

In-Service School. On May 8, 1937, all state police officers went to headquarters to attend an in-service school to undergo motorcycle training. Pictured is the entire state police department with Governor Tingley (in front, in white hat). The men in civilian clothes at right are the state police board members. These motorcycles replaced the patrol cars, but three cars were retained at headquarters to be used by the chief and plainclothes officers.

State Police Flag. Sgt. James Strosnider is seen with the new state police flag in 1938. Strosnider designed the flag and the state police collar insignias that are worn by the state police to this day.

Jack House. Jack House, son of Chief E.J. House, is seen standing between Patrolman K.K. Miller (left) and his father at the Eastern Fair in Roswell in 1937.

Chevrolet Patrol Car, 1938. This patrol unit was the first car with the official state police license plate. Before 1938, the units used the official plate that all state government vehicles used. Each car would have a unit number on the tag, along with the words "state police." The cars now had a door and trunk decal made into the shape of the state police badge. This style of door decal is still used on New Mexico State Police patrol cars. The decal was designed by Sergeant Strosnider. (Both, courtesy of K.K. Miller.)

HYDE PARK SKI BASIN. In 1938, the Hyde Park Ski Basin in Santa Fe was opened to the public. Actress Vivien Leigh attended the dedication ceremony. Shown here are, from left to right, Patrolmen C.S. McCasland and Turk Griffith, Leigh, and Patrolmen Joe Quintana and K.K. Miller.

MADGE HIGGINS. Madge Higgins was the first civilian hired by the state police. She was employed as a stenographer at $125 a month, working in the office from 8:00 a.m. to 4:00 p.m. This would relieve a patrolman from having to work in the office during the day. Madge left the state police on August 31, 1941.

CLEANING WEAPONS. Patrolmen are seen at headquarters cleaning weapons from the armory in 1938. Shown are, from left to right, Sgt. A.B. Martinez, and Patrolmen James Roach, George Day, and Jim Graham. (Courtesy of K.K. Miller.)

THE MILES BROTHERS. On the left is Patrolman Lloyd Miles, hired by the state police in 1939. On the motorcycle is his twin brother, Floyd Miles. Lloyd left the state police in 1941 to go into the US Army. Floyd joined the state police in 1941 and retired in 1982, rising to the rank of major. Brothers were not allowed to serve together in the state police in 1941. (Courtesy of Lloyd Miles.)

Blizzard in New Mexico. There was a blizzard between Lamy and Clines Corners on US 285 in January 1939. Patrolmen K.K. Miller and James Roach were stranded 12 miles north of Clines Corners for 24 hours. They walked to Clines Corners after spending the night in their car. It took nine hours to make the walk. Patrolman Miller is seen here digging out a highway department truck.

State Champions. The New Mexico State Police started the department's first pistol team in 1938. The team won the state pistol championships for 1938–1939. Lined up here are, from left to right, Sgt. Penn Winston, Capt. Jack Nichols, Patrolman C.S. McCasland, Sgt. Jim Strosnider, Patrolman James Roach, and Sgt. Al Hathaway.

State Fair Dedication. At the 1939 New Mexico State Fair, the state police were present in force at the racetrack.

New Mexico State Fair. State police officers were assigned to work security at all of the New Mexico state fairs, from the beginning in 1938 to the present time. Pictured here in 1939 are Patrolmen Frank Mann (left) and K.K. Miller. (Courtesy of K.K. Miller.)

Three

Law Enforcement During a World War

In mid-1941, before American involvement in World War II, the State of New Mexico was preparing for war. On April 16, the legislature created the New Mexico Mounted Patrol. This was a volunteer agency that would supply manpower and work with the state police in emergency situations. The mounted patrol is still in existence.

On September 10, 1941, New Mexico would undertake the first statewide civilian mobilization test in the nation. It took place on the Santa Fe–Albuquerque highway. A blackout warning would be called as Army bombers from the Albuquerque air base would quarter the state in a simulated wartime invasion. The state police would give a warning, and all traffic on the highway would stop and motorists would turn their headlights off. The state police found out during the test that sirens could not be heard, so, two days later, they repeated the test by using tracers fired from .45 automatic pistols. The shots would be fired in the air, forming a V shape.

During the early part of the war, President Roosevelt requested that all state governors take steps to set a 40-mile-per-hour speed limit to save tire wear. On March 17, 1942, New Mexico set a speed limit. Before that, the state had a "reasonable and proper" limit for cars.

There was gas and rubber rationing in the state. To enforce the speed limits, patrolmen would report speeders to the local rationing board so that they would not be able to get more tires.

By the end of 1944, twelve state policemen were on leave of absence, having enlisted or been drafted to serve in the military. Two of the state policemen died in action overseas.

During 1943, the department started researching two-way radios for the patrol cars. Due to money restraints and following much research, the proposed system went to bid on July 20, 1945. A bid was accepted from Motorola. Finally, on March 11, 1946, the first state police radio station went on the air.

Chief Tom Summers. Governor Miles took office on January 1, 1939. He appointed a rancher and former sheriff from Catron County as chief of the New Mexico State Police. Summers was the first chief appointed from outside the department. He served as chief until December 31, 1942.

Hands Across the Border. In 1940, Sgt. James Strosnider is seen greeting Capt. Manuel Labastida of the Garrison at Las Palomas, Chihuahua, Mexico.

New Mexico/Texas State Line. In 1940, members of the New Mexico State Police and the Texas Highway Patrol meet at the state line in Anthony, New Mexico. Shown here are, from left to right, Sgt. Charlie Eagleton, Capt. Carlos Salas, and Sgt. James Strosnider of New Mexico, and Texas patrolmen Carl Lovelace and Charles Reeves.

Blackout Practice. On September 12, 1941, Chief Summers (left) and Captain Martinez are seen on a hill outside of Santa Fe firing tracers to start the first blackout drill in New Mexico.

Pioneer Days Parade. On July 4, 1941, the state police escort the First Annual Pioneer Days Parade in Clovis, New Mexico.

United States Coronado Exposition. In July 1941, the state of New Mexico celebrated the 400th anniversary of the Coronado exploration of New Mexico. This is a publicity photograph from that celebration in Albuquerque.

New Mackinaws. These state police officers are showing off their new winter mackinaws in 1941. Pictured are, from left to right, Patrolman James Roach, Sgt. A.B. Martinez, Sgt. Charlie Eagleton, Sgt. James Strosnider, and Patrolmen John Bradford, Turk Griffith, Joe Quintana, and Joe Black.

Department Photograph. In 1941, the entire state police department is lined up for a dress uniform portrait. The supervisors are on the right of the photograph.

Play Day. Members of the state police are seen posing on the dunes at White Sands National Monument during the White Sands Play Day in 1941. (Courtesy of Doe Sales.)

Enlisting. On October 31, 1942, Patrolmen Ernest "Tuffy" Tafoya (center) and Grover "Jerry" Brunk enlisted in the US Navy to serve in World War II. They are shown being sworn in by an unidentified Navy recruiter.

FIELD EQUIPMENT BULLETIN. This is a page from the *New Mexico State Police Biennial Report* for 1941–1942. It lists all of the equipment that the officers were issued in 1942.

STATE POLICE OFFICERS FIELD EQUIPMENT

1. Equipment carried on person: .45 caliber Colt revolver, Sam Brown belt and holster, gold plated cap and breast badges, police whistle and cord, belt cartridge loop for 10 rounds of extra revolver ammunition, and tear gas billy.
2. Complete uniform consisting of shirts, breeches, boots, cap, leather jacket, raincoat, rubber galoshes, rubber cap cover, mackinaw, dress tunic, gloves and ties.
3. Automobiles complete with one red spotlight on right cowl, one clear spotlight on left cowl, siren, first aid kit, fire extinguisher, axe, shovel, tow chain, mud chains, hydraulic jack, flashlights, flares, red flags and police portable STOP sign. All cars are painted black, insignia of the State Police shield on both sides, grey stripe from front of radiator to rear fenders and lettered State Police on rear of body.
4. Motorcycles complete with first aid kit, fire extinguisher, siren, red spotlights. Painted silver with lettering on tanks and front of windshield.

The New Mexico State Policeman, Automobile and Motor Equipment.

New Mexico State Police

OATH OF ALLEGIANCE

to the

United States of America -- State of New Mexico

and

OATH OF OFFICE

to the

DEPARTMENT OF

NEW MEXICO STATE POLICE

I, WILLIAM T. SPEIGHT do solemnly swear that I am a citizen of the United States of America and that I am more than twenty-one years of age. That I have never been convicted of any crime, never have been dishonorably discharged from the United States Military or Naval Service or National Guard.

I do further solemnly swear that I will support and defend the Constitution of the United States of America, and the Constitution of this State, against all enemies, foreign and domestic, that I will bear true faith and allegiance to the same; that I will faithfully enforce the laws of this State and discharge the duties of the office to which I have been appointed, as a member of the New Mexico State Police, to the best of my ability and will preserve, protect and defend the honor and traditions of the New Mexico State Police, obeying all rules and regulations and carrying out all orders which may be lawfully given me by my superior officers.

Oath taken in presence of:

Chief, New Mexico State Police

The above Oath of Allegiance and Oath of Office sworn and subscribed to before me, this 28 day of January in the Year of Our Lord 1943, at Santa Fe, New Mexico.

Notary Public

My Commission Expires July 9, 1946.

OATH OF ALLEGIANCE. During World War II, members of the New Mexico State Police were required to sign an Oath of Allegiance to the United States and to the State of New Mexico. This one was signed by Patrolman William Speight on January 28, 1943.

Chief Frank Young. On January 1, 1943, former Roswell police chief Frank Young was appointed chief of the state police. He felt that the department was too rank heavy, so he demoted all supervisors to the rank of patrolman and required new supervisors to be promoted on their merit. In April 1943, Chief Young changed the uniform regulations, allowing patrolmen to wear slacks in the summertime.

Motorcycle Training. In 1943, Patrolmen Fidel Gonzales (left) and Mackie C de Baca show off their skills in the art of motorcycle riding. They are using the old 1934 motor patrol motorcycles. (Courtesy of Albert Gonzales Sr.)

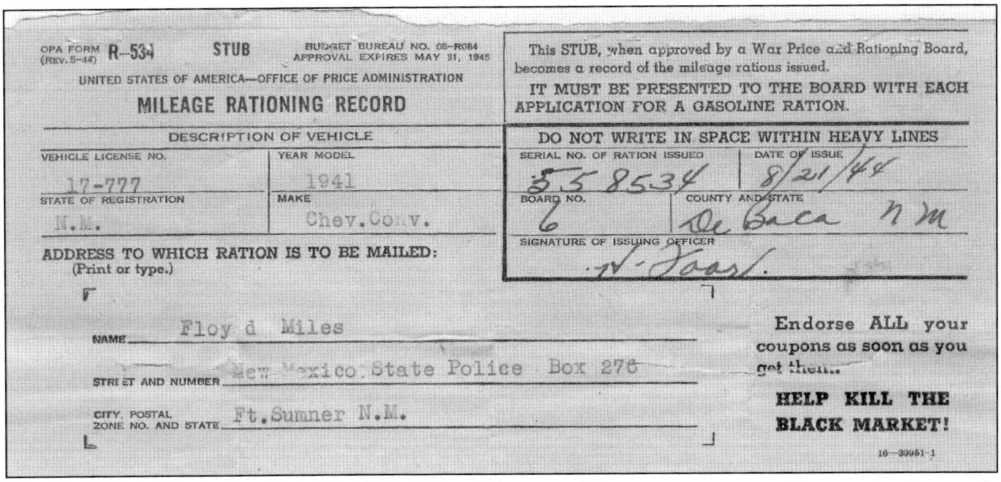

OPA FORM R-534 (REV. 5-44) STUB BUDGET BUREAU NO. 08-R084 APPROVAL EXPIRES MAY 31, 1945

UNITED STATES OF AMERICA—OFFICE OF PRICE ADMINISTRATION

MILEAGE RATIONING RECORD

This STUB, when approved by a War Price and Rationing Board, becomes a record of the mileage rations issued.

IT MUST BE PRESENTED TO THE BOARD WITH EACH APPLICATION FOR A GASOLINE RATION.

DESCRIPTION OF VEHICLE

VEHICLE LICENSE NO.	YEAR MODEL
17-777	1941
STATE OF REGISTRATION	MAKE
N.M.	Chev.Conv.

DO NOT WRITE IN SPACE WITHIN HEAVY LINES

SERIAL NO. OF RATION ISSUED	DATE OF ISSUE
558534	8/21/44
BOARD NO.	COUNTY AND STATE
6	De Baca N M

SIGNATURE OF ISSUING OFFICER

ADDRESS TO WHICH RATION IS TO BE MAILED: (Print or type.)

NAME Floy d Miles

STREET AND NUMBER New Mexico State Police Box 276

CITY, POSTAL ZONE NO. AND STATE Ft. Sumner N.M.

Endorse ALL your coupons as soon as you get them.

HELP KILL THE BLACK MARKET!

16—39951-1

GAS RATION CARD. The citizens of the United States of America were issued gas-rationing cards during World War II. The members of the state police were no exception. This is the card issued to Patrolman Floyd Miles of Ft. Sumner, New Mexico, for his personal vehicle.

WINTER 1944. The state police conducted an in-service school at headquarters in the winter of 1944. Here, the entire force is lined up with members' patrol cars.

Killed in Action. In 1944, two members of the state police were killed while on active duty with the military. Lt. Joe Quintana (above) of the US Army Air Corps was killed in England on March 21 when the plane he was piloting crashed. Pvt. Mackie C. de Baca (left) was killed in action on December 21 while serving as an Army wireman in Europe.

Patrolman Floyd Miles. Patrolman Floyd Miles joined the state police in 1941 and was stationed in Fort Sumner. Miles retired from the state police in 1982, having risen to the rank of major. Luckily for historians, he saved much of his early paperwork and memorabilia. (Courtesy of Floyd Miles.)

New Radio System. In early 1943, a two-way radio system was being considered for the state police. In September 1945, Patrolman K.K. Miller conducted a radio survey with an engineer from Motorola. In this photograph, they are on Sandia Crest, outside of Albuquerque.

First Radio Car. Patrolman Jerry Brunk had the first state police radio car. In 1946, thirty-six cars were outfitted with the new radio.

First Radio Operator. In April 1946, the first radio operator, World War II veteran and Bataan survivor Jesus Silva, was hired to work the new radio at headquarters in Santa Fe. He retired from the state police after serving for nearly 24 years.

Chief Homer Ledbetter. On January 1, 1946, Homer Ledbetter, a retired US Army colonel, was appointed chief of the state police. On October 22, 1946, Chief Ledbetter was killed in an automobile accident in Northern New Mexico while returning from a hunting trip.

Chief Hubert Beasley. On December 1, 1946, Hubert Beasley, a rancher and former sheriff from Tucumcari, was appointed chief of the state police. Chief Beasley left the department on September 30, 1950.

State Police Patrol Car. This is a state police patrol car in 1947. There was a red spotlight in front; the red light on the rear bumper was unauthorized. The gray stripes on the door and over the hood were designed by Sergeant Strosnider in the late 1930s. They are still in use today, minus the stripes on the hood.

Suspect Captured. In 1949, Patrolman John Ramsey apprehended an escaped convict after a gun battle and a fight. Ramsey is seen here escorting the wounded convict.

Four

Traffic Safety in the 1950s

Following problems caused by the appointment of a state police chief from outside the department, the 1953 legislative session passed a law whereby all state police chiefs must be appointed from within the ranks of the department. They must have served at least seven years as a commissioned officer, two of which must have been as a supervisor. Over the years, up to the present time, some state representatives have tried to do away with the law, but it has held fast.

In the early 1950s, Chief Joseph Roach started a traffic safety campaign following the rise in vehicular fatalities. The department worked hand in hand with the National Safety Council on this project. To better enforce traffic regulations, radar speed meters were purchased and sent to each state police district. To help with better enforcement and service calls, the department worked with the state legislature for a manpower increase. The state police went from 45 commissioned officers in 1950 to 150 in 1958. At the beginning of the decade, there were only three state police radio stations, and most radio traffic was handled through local police and sheriff's departments. By the end of the decade, several more New Mexico State Police radio stations were opened.

An early state police aircraft, a Cessna 180, was acquired in 1956. It was furnished to the department by the State Corporation Commission. Patrolman Melvin McGuire was appointed the first state police pilot.

During this time period, the state police temporarily changed, for the first time, part of the uniform. In 1956, due to the units not having air-conditioning and ties being worn year-round, the officers voted for a new summer uniform shirt. It was a light gray shirt with black oxford gray trim on the epaulets and shirt pocket flaps. In April 1958, another vote resulted in doing away with the gray shirt, reverting back to the regular uniform shirt.

Chief Joseph Roach. Joseph Roach became chief of the state police on October 5, 1950. He was the first chief chosen from inside the force since the tenure of Chief House. Chief Roach served in that capacity until June 1, 1959. He was commissioned into the state police on May 29, 1935.

Siege at the Penitentiary. State police stand by during an 18-hour siege by inmates at the state penitentiary in Santa Fe on December 8, 1952.

ALBUQUERQUE DISTRICT. Personnel stationed in Albuquerque pose after a meeting on March 1, 1952. The civilians in front are, from left to right, Meliton Sandoval, Grace Mounday, and Frank Wallace. The patrolmen standing in the back row are, from left to right, Eddie Apodaca, Russ Meyer, Alfred "Red" Dow, Don Novak, Mims Lane, Eddie Trujillo, Lonnie Dennis, Bill Hastings, Jack Salter, Earl Scroggins, and Bill Driggers.

IMPOUNDING VOTING BALLOTS. It was, and still is, a state law that the state police impound and guard voting ballots if requested to do so by the district attorney's office. Here, on November 5, 1952, the ballots are impounded in Gallup. The state police are, from left to right, Capt. Robert Scroggins, Patrolmen Arnold Payne and Don Shultz, unidentified, Sgt. Bud South, Patrolmen Leo Teague and Carlos Salas, and unidentified.

MEETING AT THE STATE LINE. Patrolman Eddie Jaramillo meets with officers of the Colorado State Patrol at the state line near Raton, New Mexico, around 1953. The discussion concerned traffic safety between the two states.

CAPT. JOHN BRADFORD. Bradford stands next to a patrol car in 1953. He had joined the state police in 1937 and rose to the rank of chief of the department. Here he is as a district commander.

Patrolman Carlos Salas. Carlos Salas poses next to his patrol car in 1953 on Highway 60 near his duty station of Mountainair. Salas was one of the original members of the New Mexico Motor Patrol in 1933.

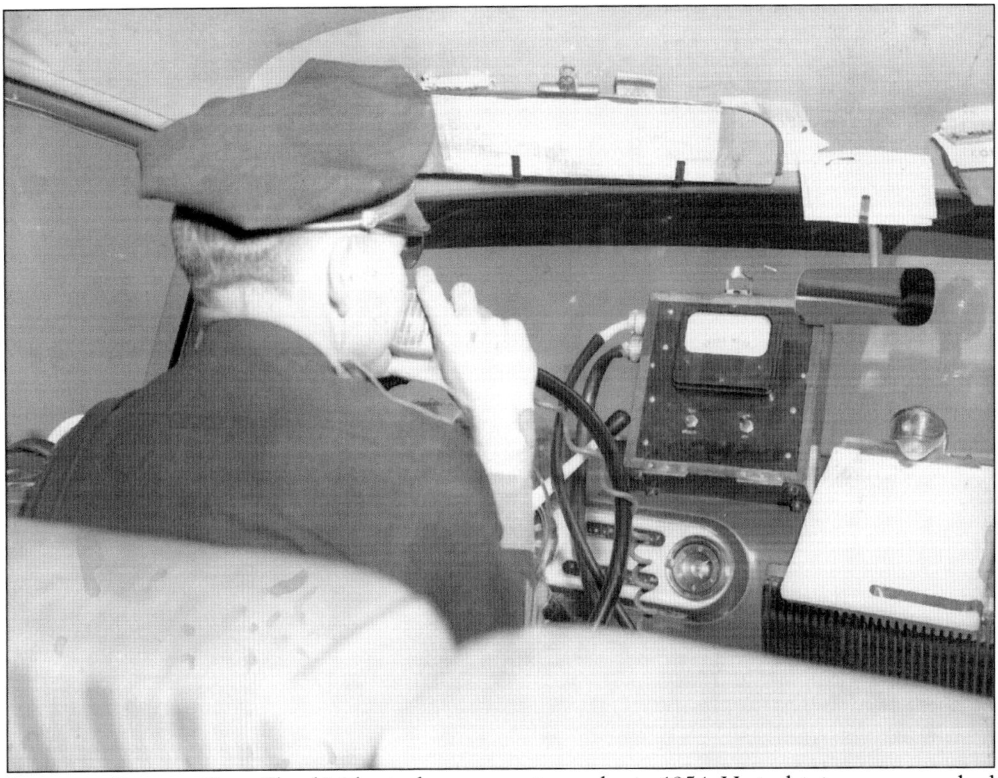

Running Radar. Capt. Floyd Miles is shown running radar in 1954. He is driving an unmarked radar car and calling in the speeds to marked units stationed down the road.

Recruit Class No. 9. The New Mexico State Police (NMSP) class No. 9 is shown here on its graduation day, October 7, 1955. In those days, the recruits did not graduate in uniform. Their first uniforms came from other officers. In fact, recruits were not told if they made the state police until the day of graduation, when their families were there to watch the event. Only then were the names read off.

Defensive Tactics. Members of NMSP class No. 9 practice defensive tactics on September 7, 1955. The school was held at St. Michael's College in Santa Fe.

Patrolman/Pilot Melvin McGuire. In 1958, the state police acquired its first aircraft, a Cessna 180 on loan from the State Corporation Commission (SCC). The first pilot, Melvin McGuire, graduated from state police school on August 15, 1949, as an enforcement officer with the SCC. He was appointed a state policeman on March 27, 1951.

Installing the Radio. Patrolman Finis Roberts is shown helping to install a radio in his new patrol car in 1956. Officers assisted automobile and radio personnel with the installation of equipment when they were issued a new unit.

Sgt. Carrol McCasland. This is Sgt. McCasland with his .357 Colt Trooper. He had joined the state police on February 10, 1937, and was known throughout his career for his skillful pistol shooting. When old-timers discuss NMSP legends, his name is among the first to be brought up.

New Uniform Shirts. In 1958, the state police officers of Lordsburg/Deming/Silver City are seen wearing the summer shirt that was issued from May 1956 until April 1958. These were the first shirts on which officers were required to wear a patch on both shoulders. Lined up here are, from left to right, Capt. Penn Winston, Sgt. Ed Bell, and Patrolmen Joe Rutland, Guy Dunivan, Jim Dahlin, and Billie Miller.

Arizona Meets New Mexico. This publicity photograph shows the cooperation between Arizona and New Mexico in their efforts to mitigate the rising accident rate. New Mexico State Police patrolman Oran Sanders is seen shaking the hand of an Arizona highway patrolman on US60 in 1956.

Headquarters Radio. A dispatcher is seen working the radio at headquarters in 1956. The radio was manned 24 hours a day. The only other radio station the state police had, set up in Alamogordo, covered the southern part of the state.

Patrolman Monroe Alexander. Patrolman Alexander stands by his 1958 Chevy patrol car in Santa Fe. He was commissioned on November 2, 1953, and retired as a captain at headquarters. In 1961, the units were changed to solid white. (Courtesy of Monroe Alexander.)

Chief Penn Wintson. Chief Winston was commissioned on the state police in the first police class on May 29, 1935. He served as chief from June 1, 1959, until March 19, 1961. He retired on March 31, 1971.

Five

Civil Disorder in the 1960s and 1970s

With the rising problem of narcotic use and distribution, the state police saw a need to form a narcotics section. In late 1960, a patrolman was assigned as a state police narcotics agent. He turned in his marked unit and was given an unmarked black-and-white with a whip antenna.

In 1962, the recruit training school was moved from St. Michael's College to the Glorieta Baptist Assembly and was changed from four to six weeks in length. By 1966, the department had 236 commissioned officers.

In late 1963, the department created the Special Investigations Division, placing 10 investigators in that division. As protests and riots began increasing around the country and several underground organizations were being established to undermine government agencies, the state police would send agents of the intelligence division into college campuses to document information concerning upcoming criminal events.

In 1963, the department created the official underwater recovery team, which used modern diving equipment and methods of operation. Before that, local officers conducted rescue and recovery missions.

The 1968 state legislature approved funding for the design, construction, and equipping of a new state police headquarters complex and law enforcement academy in Santa Fe. The construction of the complex commenced in 1969 and was completed in 1970. The 28th recruit school started its training in Glorieta and was the first recruit school to graduate from the new academy.

In 1971, the department switched back to the traditional black-and-white patrol cars. Also that year, a 1971 Cessna Skymaster 337 twin-engine airplane replaced the old aircraft that had been put into commission in 1956.

During the early 1970s, students at colleges and universities throughout the country were involved in riots to protest US policies on the Vietnam War. Riots occurred at the University of New Mexico and New Mexico State University, and officers from the field were sent in to handle the problems. The need was recognized to train a tactical team made up of officers throughout the state to respond to riots.

Chief Kenneth K. Miller. Kenneth Miller was promoted to chief of the state police on March 20, 1961. He had joined the department on April 23, 1937, as a patrolman/mechanic. As the Harley-Davidson dealer in Albuquerque in 1933, Miller sold the motor patrol its motorcycles. He retired on December 31, 1968.

New Weapons. Chief Miller is seen in 1961 trying out the new M16 automatic rifle. The department bought two of these weapons, and they are still in the state police inventory.

Vice President Hubert Humphrey. In 1964, vice presidential hopeful Hubert Humphrey is seen in Santa Fe with members of the state police. Posing with Humphrey are, from left to right, (first row) Lt. Freddie Martinez, Deputy Chief Joe Black, Capt. A.J. Smith, and Lt. M.K. Alexander; (second row) Patrolman Richard C de Baca, Lt. T.J. Chavez, Capt. Penn Winston, and Santa Fe police chief A.B. Martinez.

Dive School. The new dive team for the state police is shown here during the 1964 dive school. Before a team was formed, local officers would respond to a drowning. Jim Syling, one of the original divers, formed up the new team. He remained in charge of the team until he retired some 20 years later.

Baton Training. In 1967, state police officers went to the Los Angeles Police Department to train in riot control using the LAPD baton. During 1967–1968, state police officers were trained in the use of baton and riot control. They were authorized to use the baton only for riot duties.

Chief John Bradford. John Bradford was promoted to chief on February 1, 1965. He had joined the state police on November 21, 1937. Chief Bradford replaced K.K. Miller, who took a demotion to captain for health reasons. The rank of chief is a temporary title; when a chief leaves that position, he or she reverts back to the rank of captain.

Security for the Gallup Indian Ceremonies. Officers from multiple agencies, including the state police, pose for a group photograph in 1966 after a briefing. The Indian ceremonies are held annually during a weekend in August. Air police from Kirkland Air Force Base in Albuquerque are also on hand to help with traffic control.

On Patrol. In 1967, Patrolmen Bob Hodges (left) and Doyle Randall take a ride on a bicycle built for two.

Chief Joseph Black. Chief Black was promoted on April 26, 1967. He joined the state police on April 16, 1939. Prior to that, he was an investigator for the motor patrol. Under his command, the rank of chief was referred to as "colonel."

Ground-Breaking Ceremony. In 1968, the local state police are lined up for the ground-breaking ceremony for the New Mexico State Police Headquarters and Law Enforcement Academy in Santa Fe.

NARCOTICS SECRETARY. This is a 1968 photograph of longtime narcotics secretary Maggie Trujillo. Looking at the cluttered office, it is easy to see why the state police had a need for a new, bigger complex.

FOOT PURSUIT. In 1969, state police officers caught a burglary suspect after a foot pursuit south of Albuquerque. The officers shown here are Patrolmen Bob Holley (left), Brent Bateman (center), and Al Leroy.

A Long Drop. In 1969, the dive team commander, Lt. Jim Syling, is seen hanging, without a safety line, 200 feet in the air. This training involved a method to quickly transport a diver to a dive mission.

Chief Martin Vigil. Martin Vigil was appointed chief on December 6, 1969, and retired on December 1, 1982. He has the distinction of being the longest-serving chief of the New Mexico State Police. Chief Vigil became a patrolman on April 1, 1947.

PLYMOUTH, 1970. This is the 1970 Plymouth Fury I patrol car. It was one of the first state police units to have the double red lights. One of the lights had a motor, and the other one rotated by a chain that was attached to the other light and ran through the middle bar.

ALBUQUERQUE RIOTS. In the early 1970s, antiwar riots occurred on the University of New Mexico campus. Over 80 police officers responded. Protestors are seen here following their arrest, escorted by Patrolman Juan Chavez and Lt. Don Moberly at the top of the stairs and Patrolman Jim Butler, third from the left facing the camera. The other officers are state policemen and mounted patrolmen.

WEAPONS DISPLAY. At the 1970 Home Show in Santa Fe, a state police unit is set up with a display of weapons that were available to the officers.

PATROLMAN RUBEN VIRAMONTES. Patrolman Viramontes is seen here with his 1969 Plymouth Fury in May 1970. When patrol cars traveled at high speeds, the red-light bar would vibrate. On this bar, another metal bar has been attached to add weight in an attempt to cut down on the vibration.

Silver Grips Award. In the early 1970s, the state police gave awards to officers who recovered the most stolen cars. The award recipients were categorized by those who worked less-traveled roads and those who patrolled interstates. On February 5, 1971, Patrolman Bob Welborn (left), pictured with his wife, Sherry, receives the Silver Grips award from Chief Vigil for recovering 28 stolen cars on less-traveled roads in 1970.

Sgt. Bill Eddleman. State police pilot Bill Eddleman stands in front of Aircraft 544 in 1970 in Santa Fe.

PLYMOUTH FURY, 1971. This is the first black-and-white unit after the state police decided to revert to the traditional scheme. The state police units are still black-and-white. On top of this car, tennis balls are wedged between the bar and the roof to cut down on the bar's vibration.

STATE POLICE HEADQUARTERS. The new State Police Headquarters and Law Enforcement Academy at Santa Fe was completed in 1970. On the bottom right is the District One office, and on the left is the unpaved driving track. The state police still use this headquarters.

SM-7 CLASS. In 1971, all state police commissioned officers attended a class and were certified on the new "Balloon Test," the Sober-Meter Mobat breath test for suspected drunk drivers. Every one of the old-timers can describe the Mobat Twist. This test was used into the mid-1980s.

K-9 THOR. In 1971, Agent Dean Stuyvesant shows off Thor, the state police's first K-9 dog, during an event in Santa Fe.

State Police Air Detail. Due to an increase in the use of aircraft in narcotics smuggling, an air detail was formed by the state police narcotics division. Pictured on February 22, 1972, the charter members of the Narcotics Air Intelligence Detail are, from left to right, Lynn Heimerich, Neil Curran, Willie Garcia, Bill Eddleman, and D.C. Jackson.

Northern Tactical Team. Because of the unrest on college campuses in New Mexico, the state police formed a tactical team to deal with the riots instead of sending in uniformed officers from the field. Seen here is the Northern Team during training in Santa Fe in 1973.

Dive Team at Tesuque Lake. On July 3, 1973, the Search and Recovery Team conducted test diving at Tesuque Lake in Northern New Mexico. The divers are, from left to right, Lt. Jim Syling, Patrolman Robert Trippeer, Sgt. Bill Holder, Lt. Paul Gregory, Patrolman John Smith, and state police commissioner Mahlon Love. Commissioner Love, a civilian, paid his own way to attend the 30th Recruit School in 1972.

Lockdown. Because of a strike by prison employees in Santa Fe in 1972, the state police tactical team operated the state penitentiary for 24 hours. Seen here are Patrolmen Ken Riedemann (left) and John McAninch.

Drip Gas Detail. Due to a rise in thefts of drip gas from oil wells in the northwest part of New Mexico, the state police formed a drip gas detail, made up of officers stationed in Farmington. Pictured here with their units in 1975 are Patrolmen Richard Rush (left), Bob Hodges (center), and Jim Hiltsley.

Traffic Enforcement. Because of the gas shortage, a national maximum speed limit of 55 miles per hour was established in 1974. New Mexico State Police set up aircraft speed enforcement and stopwatch zones on all of the interstates. Here, a patrolman in Santa Fe in 1975 issues a speeding citation to a motorist clocked in an aircraft zone.

OFFICER SAFETY TRAINING. At the 1976 in-service school in Santa Fe, Patrolman Larry Allen, kneeling, participates in an exercise teaching the proper and safe way to make a felony traffic stop.

WOMEN ON THE STATE POLICE. The first women to join the New Mexico State Police graduated from class No. 34 on October 1, 1976. The trailblazing women were Patrolmen Dorcus "Charlie" Bailey and Sue DeWalt.

Pistol Team. The state police pistol team was one of the best in New Mexico. Here, the four-man team gathers after competing in a match in 1976. The team members are, from left to right, Patrolmen Don Helberg, Jerry Williams, Bill Butts, and Sgt. Bobby Miller.

Bicentennial License Plate. In 1976, to honor the bicentennial celebration, the state police designed a license plate for the department's marked units. These plates remained on the units into the early 1990s. The plate is colored blue with red letters and border. The Zia sun symbol is yellow with red lettering. (Courtesy of Norman Rhoades.)

Six

The 1980s and a New State Police

The New Mexico State Penitentiary riot on February 2, 1980, will be remembered as the worst in state history. The prison was in the hands of rampaging inmates for 36 hours. The prisoners burned the penitentiary, causing nearly $22 million in damages and taking the lives of 33 inmates. The State Police Tactical Team and other state police officers were at the penitentiary throughout the riot. The National Guard and many local law enforcement officers from around the state were also on duty in Santa Fe during the event.

The 1980s saw an influx of illegal contraband smuggled across New Mexico. In 1983, the state police seized over $239 million worth of cocaine, primarily by traffic stops on Interstate 40. They also confiscated $1.6 million in drug-related cash. As a result of this excellent work, some officers were asked to conduct training sessions throughout the United States.

During 1987, the department was about to undergo a structural change that would not be an easy transition for many of the members. As Gov. Gary Carruthers took office, he began a state government consolidation program that combined several state entities under one organization headed by a cabinet secretary. The proposed department was to be called the Public Safety Department; eventually, the name was changed to the Department of Public Safety (DPS).

Under this system, the DPS comprised several agencies, including the New Mexico State Police, Department of Alcohol Beverage Control, Civil Emergency Preparedness, Division of the Office of Military Affairs, and the New Mexico Law Enforcement Academy.

In 1984, a state police tradition was broken when the department allowed officers to wear short-sleeved shirts during the summer months. Prior to this, officers were limited to long-sleeved shirts without the tie in the summer. It was not mandatory for officers to wear the short sleeves, and some chose to wear long sleeves year-round.

The state police ventured from another tradition in 1989 by employing six unmarked units, outfitted with the new HAWK radar, to patrol strategic locations throughout New Mexico. The stealth units, as they became known, were multicolored slick-tops.

STATE FAIR, 1980. Lt. Finis Roberts briefs the officers assigned to work the 1980 State Fair in Albuquerque.

THE FIRST SLICK-TOP UNIT. In 1981, District Four patrolman Don Morrison conducted a four-month evaluation of a slick-top unit in Las Cruces. He took the red lights off of his car and, with the help of state policemen Eddie Espinoza and Ron Taylor and Texas highway patrolman Bob Collins, outfitted the unit. Soon after, slick-top units were authorized for the state police.

Richard C de Baca. Chief C de Baca served as chief of the state police from December 1, 1982, to February 11, 1983. After C de Baca retired, he became the cabinet secretary for the Department of Public Safety in 1991. He was commissioned on the state police on July 1, 1956. (Courtesy of Richard C de Baca.)

Mustang Testing. In January 1983, the Ford Company loaned a 1982 Mustang to the state police to determine if the department wanted to purchase some units. The car, painted and licensed to make it official, was assigned to several districts on the interstates for testing. The plan to purchase several Mustangs was turned down because officers preferred their larger cars.

Chief Maurice Cordova. Chief Cordova was promoted to the rank of chief on March 4, 1983, to replace Chief C de Baca. Cordova had joined the state police on November 2, 1953.

Capt. I.B. Pickett. Captain Pickett, seen here as a deputy chief, was for years in charge of the department's fleet of vehicles. During that time, the officers referred to their units as "Pickett's Cars." An officer who wrecked or abused a unit knew that Captain Pickett would more than likely never issue him a new car again. Do not wreck Pickett's Cars!

State Police Dive Team. The dive team is seen here during training in 1981. Pictured are, from left to right, Mason Warren, Jim Syling, Marshall Warren, Jim Allison, John Smith, Don Rehm, Curtis Harding, Steve Swingle, Tom Hawkins, Bob Trippeer, Duel Paris, Andy Benavidez, Phil Snedeker, Ed Yeager, Al Leroy, Robbie Coon, Lonnie Valencia, and Jack Jones.

Explosives Disposal Team. The formation of an explosives disposal team was initiated by the department in 1981, following an attempted bombing of the Espanola state police office. Shown here in 1984 are, from left to right, (first row) Agents Pete Ross, Mike Francis, and Roger Payne, and Patrolman Norman Rhoades; (second row) Patrolman Bill Hanson, Michael Bell (Crime Lab), Patrolmen John Reynolds and Lonnie Valencia, and Sgt. Leo Martinez.

Meeting at the State Line. In 1984, Las Cruces District Four officers meet Texas highway patrolmen at the state line in Anthony, New Mexico, to recreate the meeting in 1940 (see page 43). This was for the state police 50th anniversary yearbook. Pictured here are, from left to right, Sgt. Ron Baker and Patrolmen Eddie Espinoza and Rudy Ramirez of the New Mexico State Police, and Sgt. Bob Collins and Trooper Randall Messick of the Texas Highway Patrol.

Chief Maurice Payne. Chief Payne was promoted to that rank on September 1, 1985. Payne was commissioned on the state police on April 1, 1958.

HONOR GUARD. The State Police Honor Guard was formed on July 1, 1984, to provide a service during funerals of commissioned officers, retired officers, or elected officials. The guard is used in the event of visiting dignitaries or during occasions deemed appropriate by the chief of the New Mexico State Police.

HELICOPTER TRAINING. In 1984, two members of the tactical team are seen rappelling from the state police helicopter during annual training.

State Police Golden Anniversary. In 1985, the New Mexico State Police celebrated its 50th anniversary in several ways. One was a float, which participated in every major parade in the state that year. Seen here in the Las Cruces Harvest Festival Parade are tactical team member Frank De la O and dive team member Travis Johnson. The float took second place in the parade.

Golden Anniversary Painting. In 1985, to help celebrate the golden anniversary of the state police, Farmington artist Randy Follis created a painting that showed the state police at work over those 50 years. The depiction of the officer next to the motorcycle is based on a photograph of Patrolman Penn Winston in 1935, and the model for the modern officer is Patrolman Mason Warren.

Drug Money Recovered. Patrolman Nathan Wallace, who was stationed in Tucumcari, poses with a $1.5-million cash seizure related to illegal drug trafficking that he recovered on a traffic stop in 1985.

Headquarters Dispatch Center. Seen here in 1985 are two of the headquarters communication specialists, Robert Patton and Pat Caldwell. Each state police district has its own dispatch center, but in emergencies, headquarters has the ability to make radio contact with any police unit in the state.

Photo Opportunity. These officers, who were in Santa Fe for an in-service school session, are lined up with new patrol cars for a photograph to appear in the golden anniversary yearbook in 1985.

Chopper Crash. This customs helicopter crashed on a mission in Chavez County on August 29, 1986. The chopper developed mechanical problems during a drug raid. Tactical team members Jerry Urban, Pat Wood, and Robbie Coon were seriously injured. Bomb team commander Sgt. Pete Ross broke his back and was medically retired from the state police. (Courtesy of Robert Perkins.)

New State Police District. In 1984, District 16 was added to the list of state police districts. This district, in the southwest part of the state, covers Deming, Lordsburg, and Silver City. Pictured here in 1984 after a weapons qualification are the officers stationed in Lordsburg. They are, from left to right, patrol officers Ron Mullins, Mike French, Roxanna McGahey, and Mark Clayton.

Chief Neil Curran. Chief Curran was appointed chief on July 31, 1987. He graduated from recruit school on November 6, 1965. (Courtesy of Neil Curran.)

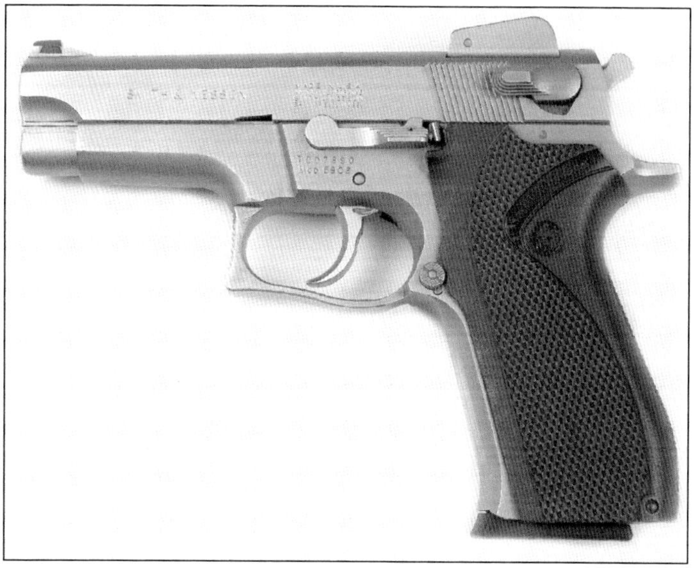

Semiautomatic Pistol. On October 17, 1988, members of Recruit School No. 47 were trained on and issued the new Smith & Wesson 9 mm Model 5906 pistol, replacing the .357 revolvers that had been carried by the commissioned officers of the state police. It was a very unpopular weapon among officers, and before the full department completed the transition, the pistol was replaced with the S&W .45 Model 4506.

Marijuana Field. On August 14, 1989, the state police, assisted by several law enforcement agencies, raided a large marijuana plantation outside of Tucumcari. The investigation was led by members of the NMSP Narcotics Division. The US Air Force assisted by taking high-level photographs of the plantation. Here, Patrolman Larry Hines demonstrates the plants' height.

Seven

The Modern State Police

In June 1990, the state police finally adopted the Ford Mustang as a speed-enforcement unit. The goal was to cut down traffic fatalities and enforce speed limits, so the department put six Mustangs on the road throughout the state.

In 1991, the department started issuing AR-15 rifles to the officers. Prior to this, officers used shotguns, which were kept in the trunks of the units. If an officer wanted to carry a personal long rifle, he requested permission from headquarters and then passed a qualification test. After the AR-15 was issued, officers could choose to carry the rifle or the shotgun in their units.

On May 14, 1998, for the first time, members of the state police were awarded the Medal of Valor, Distinguished Service Medal, and the Meritorious Achievement Award. Gov. Gary Johnson presented the awards to the officers. Earlier, in 1995, the families of state policemen who were killed in the line of duty were given the newly designed Medal of Valor.

Also in 1998, a special legislative session was called in the spring to enact a law whereby the Motor Transportation Department (MTD) was removed from under the Taxation and Revenue Department and placed within the Department of Public Safety.

In the 1990s and into the next decade, there was a nationwide push for the reduction of fatal accidents involving alcohol. New Mexico was no exception. In fact, for years it ranked among the states highest in alcohol-related accidents. The Department of Public Safety received grant money from the federal government to apply to equipment and overtime pay for officers to enforce the liquor laws, both in sales of alcohol and in terms of intoxicated driving. All of the divisions worked as a team to reduce the fatality rate.

In 2011, DPS went back to the unmarked cars, purchasing Dodge Chargers to work traffic enforcement. This was the first time that unmarked units had been employed in the force since the Mustang program in 1990.

The current authorized manpower for the state police is 567 commissioned officers. The department has come a long way from its 10 patrolmen in 1933.

STEALTH UNIT. Pictured here is a 1988 Chevrolet Caprice, used by Patrolman Norman Rhoades in District Four, Las Cruces. The department used several of these unmarked cars throughout New Mexico for traffic enforcement. Rhoades used his from 1989 to 1990. (Courtesy of Norman Rhoades.)

MUSTANG CLASS. On June 26, 1990, officers trained to take over six Ford Mustangs that were going to be used in traffic enforcement. The officers are, from left to right, (first row) Joel Ryan (instructor), Jaime Leyva, Steve Montez, Dominic Pargas, Danny Lichtenberger, and Rick Masingale; (second row) Tim Sharpe, Edward Espinoza, Michael Fousek, Tom Christian, Bobby Toler, Norman Rhoades, Santiago Hernandez, and Gabe Romero.

Mike Gibson. Pictured here is Patrolman Mike Gibson in Albuquerque, with one of two fully marked Ford Mustang patrol cars.

Rifle Transition. In 1991 and 1992, the state police held transition training for the Colt AR-15 H Bar rifle for all commissioned officers. Shown here are the officers from District Four, Las Cruces, going through the training. The instructors were Mike Gibson, Rick Durham, Robert Holguin, and Richard Newman.

Chief John Denko. Denko was promoted to chief on February 2, 1991. He was later appointed cabinet secretary for the Department of Public Safety. He was commissioned as a state police officer on December 30, 1974.

Side by Side. This photograph of a US Air Force Stealth F-117A and a 1992 state police car was taken on September 14, 1992, during an open house at Holloman Air Force Base in Alamogordo.

Chief Frank Taylor. Frank Taylor was promoted to the rank of chief on January 1, 1995. He was commissioned in the department on December 1, 1973.

Chief Carlos Maldonado. Carlos Maldonado became chief on January 1, 2003. He was commissioned as an officer on October 31, 1981.

Legislative Security. When the state legislature is in session, the New Mexico State Police provide security for the representatives and senators. Personnel are brought in from around the state for this assignment. Pictured here are the officers providing security in 2004. They are circled around the state seal in the rotunda floor of the capitol.

Katrina Relief. During the recovery efforts following Hurricane Katrina, the New Mexico State Police sent three groups to assist the city of New Orleans. Pictured here is Group B, which was there on October 6, 2005.

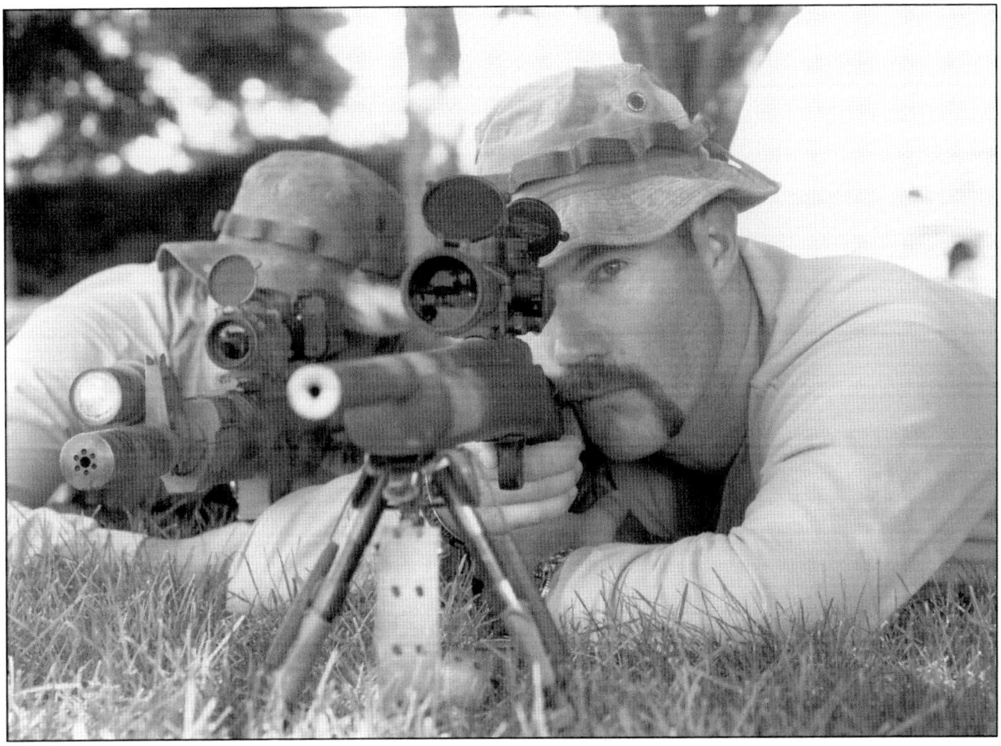

SNIPER. Pictured here is a tactical team sniper, Sgt. Kevin McPherson, with his spotter, Patrolman John Salas. This photograph was taken for the 70th anniversary yearbook. (Courtesy of Mike Trompak.)

CHIEF FARON SEGOTTA. Faron Segotta was promoted to the rank of chief on March 8, 2006. He was commissioned on the state police on October 29, 1982.

Run for the Wall. In 2010, several hundred veterans passed through New Mexico on Interstate 10 on their way to Washington, DC, and the Vietnam Veterans Memorial. NMSP officers escorted the motorcyclists through the state. Pictured here at the Arizona/New Mexico state line are, from left to right, Sgt. Guy Archuleta and Patrolmen Johnny Vijil, Scott Merrill, and Pat Kuchma. In the marked units are Sgt. Ron Taylor and Patrolmen Raul Martinez and Thomas Vitale.

Canine Team. Picture here are members of the canine team in 2005. They are, from left to right, K-9 officers James Butterfield, Patrick Gonzales, Arcenio Chavez, and Beau Johnston, Sgt. Rudy Mora, and K-9 officers Penny Ryan and Shawn Watson. (Courtesy of Mike Trompak.)

Motorcycle Unit. Members of the motor unit pose for a photograph after working a project in Las Cruces on December 13, 2012. Shown here are, from left to right, (first row) Sgt. Jeff Rey, Patrolmen Justin Davis and Johnny Vijil, Sgt. Marc Mier, and Patrolman Scott Merrill; (second row) Patrolman Orlando Sanchez, Sgt. Jose Martinez, Lt. Dominic Aragon, Sgt. Bill Thornock, and Patrolman Aaron Hammonds. (Courtesy of Scott Merrill.)

Honor Guard. The current honor guard poses in the new, retro state police uniforms and revolvers. Pictured here, not in order, are Lt. Tom Harzewski, Sgt. Rudy Rael, Sgt. Emmanuel Gutierrez, Sgt. James Jenkins, Agent Bernadette Jaramillo, Patrolmen Enrique Vega, James Dean, Dennis Lopez, Michael Smith, Spencer Roberts, Ben Swope, Ryan Gates, Adrian Salas, Santiago Grijalva, and Sergio Aranda. Not pictured is Patrolman Abel Mireles. (Courtesy of Tom Harzewski.)

EMERGENCY RESPONSE TEAM. The ERT was formed in 1997. Its duties involve crowd control and addressing civil disorder. Pictured here in 2005 are a few members with their equipment. They are, from left to right, (first row) Agent David Candelaria, Sgts. Robert Duncan and Robert Miller, and Agent Richard Mathews; (second row) Patrolman Al Quintero, Agents James Mowduk and Freddy De La O, Sgt. Tommy Hooper, and Patrolmen Tom Hicks and Steve Mulkey.

ERT TRAINING. In July 2012, several members of the ERT attended a Field Force Extrication Training course at the Center for Domestic Preparedness in Anniston, Alabama. Pictured here are, from left to right, Agent Noe Alvarado, Sgt. W. Troy Weisler, Agent Raymundo Sanchez, MTD Patrolman Carlos Perea, Patrolmen Julio Barragan and Mark Fambrough, Agent Daniel Lazos, and Patrolman Brett Jensen. (Courtesy of Troy Weisler.)

Crime Scene Team. The crime scene team was formed in 1995. Members of the team pose in 2005. They are, from left to right, Agents Paul Chavez, Joe Schiel, Richard Mathews, Shayne Arthur, Kevin Massis, and Norman Rhoades, and Sgt. Art Ortiz. (Courtesy of Norman Rhoades.)

Search and Recovery Team. Pictured here in 2005 are members of the search and recovery team during winter training in a snowstorm. They are, from left to right, (first row) Mike Waring and Gene Galassini; (second row) Dominic Pargas, Keith Elder, Jennie Pierce, Chris Boor, and Pat Garrett; (third row) Scott Weaver, Darren Holley, Jack Bratcher, Jaime Leyva, Chris Martinez, and Ben Hazen.

AIRCRAFT SECTION. Seen here posing in front of Air Unit ABLE-6 are members of the aircraft section in 2012. They are, from left to right, pilot Thomas Long, Tactical Fight Officer James Parks, pilots Victor Gallegos and Benito Pacheco, and Tactical Flight Officer Mitch Bengston. (Courtesy of Mitch Bengston.)

PISTOL TEAM. The New Mexico State Police Pistol Team is pictured on September 20, 2012, at the NRA National Police Shooting Championships in Albuquerque. Shown here are, from left to right, Agent Warren Pershall, Sgt. Kevin McPherson (retired), Patrolman Dennis Gold, Sgt. Andy Baldridge, Patrolman Thomas Lewis, Agent Elizabeth Whitfield, Patrolman Joshua Adams, and Agent Carrie McPherson. (Courtesy of Kevin McPherson.)

TACTICAL TEAM. The current tactical team poses during a training session. Shown here are, from left to right, (first row) Jorge Lopez, Richard Mathews, Jerry Saldivar, Alex Horcasitas, Jose Urbano (K-9 handler); (second row) Jonathan Tenorio, Bryan Waller, Josh Willis, Michael Williams, Hugo Munoz, Shane Todd, Joseph Chavez, Michael Gallardo, Philip Candelaria, and Ray White. (Courtesy of Sgt. Alex Horcaitas.)

BOMB TEAM. Pictured here are the current members of the bomb team with Rex the Robot. They are, from left to right, (first row) Agent Vincent Montez and Patrolmen Jose Gaytan and Albert Holguin; (second row) Agent Alfredo Aguirre, Sgt. Jose Salazar, Sgt. Leonardo Ornelas, and Patrolman Gabe Luna. (Courtesy of Amy Luna, Embrace Life Photography.)

Dodge Charger. During 2011, the state police purchased several unmarked Dodge Chargers and issued them to officers in the districts to work traffic and DWI enforcement. (Courtesy of Agent Norman Rhoades.)

Ford Fusion. In 2012, the New Mexico State Police started issuing the newest unit in the fleet, the 2012 Ford Fusion. (Courtesy of Norman Rhoades.)

Seniority on the State Police. Pictured here is Telecommunications Operator Giovanni Gardiner. Gio currently has the most seniority as a state police civilian. She was hired on January 18, 1979, and has been a dispatcher with Las Cruces, District Four, her entire career.

Retirement Day. On January 1, 2012, three senior state policemen retired from the department on the same day in District Four, Las Cruces. The retirees are, from left to right, Sgt. Ron Taylor (40 years, 3 months), Patrolman Pat Kuchma (21 years, 1 month), and Raul Martinez (18 years, 6 months with NMSP and 5 years, 6 months in other agencies). (Courtesy of Norman Rhoades.)

Chief Robert Shilling. Chief Shilling was promoted to his present rank on April 22, 2011, and is the current chief of the New Mexico State Police. He was commissioned on the department December 11, 1992. (Courtesy of Mike Trompak.)

Cabinet Secretary Gorden Eden. Secretary Eden began his career in 1975 as a NM State Police officer, which included assignments in the office of the chief. He has also served at Northwestern University, the attorney general's office, and as director of the motor vehicle division. In May 2002, he was appointed by President Bush as the 19th US Marshal for the District of New Mexico. (Courtesy of Mike Trompak.)

Eight

New Mexico State Police Officers Killed in the Line of Duty

Being a police officer in the United States is a dangerous job. The men and women who work in such an important occupation know that on any call or during any traffic stop, they could lose their lives. Police officers choose to be in law enforcement not for the money or any kind of glory. They do the work because they want to make a difference and they enjoy helping people.

In the history of the New Mexico State Police, there have been 31 officers killed in the line of duty. What many people do not realize is that there are many other state police officers that have died while off duty. Among the ranks of the NMSP, 21 officers have died or been killed while off duty, and they are mourned and missed. The officers killed in the line of duty are the ones most honored.

With this chapter, the author chooses to honor the officers who gave their final sacrifices for the citizens of New Mexico.

Patrolman Walter Taber. Patrolman Taber was stationed in Grants, having been commissioned on December 26, 1935. While leaving Santa Fe on his motorcycle, he was struck by a car. He died from his injuries six days later, on September 28, 1937.

Patrolman Jose "Joe" Quintana. Patrolman Quintana was commissioned on the state police on November 29, 1937, and was stationed in Albuquerque. During World War II, he took military leave and was commissioned as an officer/pilot in the US Army Air Corps, stationed in England. On March 21, 1944, he was killed in a plane crash in that country.

Patrolman Mackie C de Baca. Patrolman C de Baca was stationed in Santa Fe, having been commissioned on April 16, 1937. He took military leave during World War II and was serving in the US Army in Europe as a wireman. On December 21, 1944, C de Baca was killed in action.

Patrolman Leslie Delbert Bugg. Patrolman Bugg was commissioned on April 9, 1946, and was stationed in Tucumcari. On August 21, 1946, he died from injuries sustained the day before while he was riding his motorcycle on patrol on US 66 in Tucumcari. He was hit by a car that had crossed the center line.

Patrolman William Speight. Patrolman Speight was commissioned on November 20, 1937, and was stationed in Alamogordo. On February 21, 1949, he was in the Sacramento Mountains checking the state police radio tower on Wolford Mountain near Cloudcroft. He never returned. After a search, he was found deceased near the tower, having died from exposure. He used to have blackouts due to a previous gunshot wound and broken neck.

Patrolman Nash Garcia. Patrolman Garcia was stationed in Grants after he was commissioned on June 15, 1944. On April 11, 1952, he was in pursuit of a car that was occupied by two local men. When he rounded a curve, he was ambushed and shot. He was then pulled out of the car and beaten to death.

Sgt. John "Jake" Ramsey and Patrolman Joe Aven. Sergeant Ramsey (right) was commissioned on April 1, 1949. Patrolman Aven (below) was commissioned on August 15, 1949. They were stationed in Hobbs. On August 5, 1953, the two officers were driving eastbound in Texas with the Hobbs police chief in the unit with them. A car coming from the opposite direction crossed the center line and hit them head-on. Sergeant Ramsey died at the scene, and patrolman Aven died the next day.

Patrolman Robert E. Lee. Patrolman Lee, stationed in Las Cruces, was commissioned on September 7, 1955. On August 16, 1960, he was driving eastbound on US 70, east of Las Cruces, on the way to assist a stranded motorist. A vehicle parked on the shoulder made a U-turn into his path, causing the cars to collide and the unit to roll over, killing Patrolman Lee.

Capt. James Clark. Captain Clark was stationed in Clovis and had been commissioned on November 21, 1937. On September 16, 1960, he had just left Cannon Air Force Base and was driving on a back road at night. He approached a railroad crossing and hit the side of a moving train. He was killed instantly.

Patrolman Benny Williams. Patrolman Williams was stationed in Portales and was hired on May 16, 1961. On July 9, 1963, he was driving on US 70, heading to an accident scene. The roadway was wet and slick. He lost control of his patrol car, and it rolled over. Patrolman Williams died of his injuries a short time later.

Patrolman Antonio Jaramillo. Patrolman Jaramillo was stationed in Santa Rosa and had been commissioned on April 16, 1964. On January 31, 1965, he was assisting the Santa Rosa Police Department at an accident scene. Jaramillo was directing traffic when he was struck by a vehicle and injured. He died of his injuries two days later.

Agent Robert Romero. Agent Romero was assigned to the attorney general's office as an investigator. He had been commissioned on the state police July 16, 1959. On September 30, 1967 he was killed when the car he was driving rear-ended a logging truck on US 64. There was fog in the area at the time.

Patrolman Robert Rosenbloom. Patrolman Rosenbloom was stationed in Albuquerque and was commissioned on April 25, 1965. On November 8, 1971, he was working traffic on I-40 west of Albuquerque. He had just stopped a car and was shot with a .45 automatic. The suspects fled the scene and hijacked a commercial airliner in Albuquerque and were flown to Cuba.

Patrolman David Coker. Patrolman Coker was stationed in Santa Rosa. He was hired on October 1, 1975. On November 18, 1979, he was working traffic on I-40 west of Santa Rosa when he stopped a car for speeding. The driver pulled a gun on the officer and disarmed him of his duty revolver. Coker then pulled a backup weapon. Both men fired one shot, killing each other.

Patrolman Richard Gomez. Patrolman Gomez was stationed in Gallina. He was commissioned on December 1, 1970. On April 17, 1980, he made a traffic stop on a local resident for suspected drunk driving. The driver pulled a .22 pistol and shot the officer in the shoulder, severing an artery. Gomez died of that wound shortly afterward at the hospital.

Patrolman/Pilot Lowell Howard and Patrolman David Smith. Patrolman Howard (left) and Patrolman Smith (below) were commissioned together in Recruit School No. 36 on October 16, 1978. Pilot Howard was stationed in Santa Fe, and Patrolman Smith was in Farmington. On August 6, 1984, they had been working a highway traffic speed zone. Smith, a local district officer, was an observer. When the project was finished, they were landing at the airport when their plane hit power lines, causing it to crash. Both officers were killed.

Sgt. Joseph Robert Evetts. Joseph Evetts was stationed in Raton. He was commissioned on June 2, 1966. On December 24, 1982, he was clearing snow from the walkway in front of the district office when he had a heart attack and died.

Patrolman Manuel Olivas. Patrolman Olivas was stationed in Ribera. He was commissioned on December 27, 1980. On February 1, 1985, while he was out of his unit investigating an accident on I-25, an intoxicated driver struck him and left the scene. The body was discovered by a tow truck driver who had been dispatched to the accident. The drunk driver was located in a nearby motel and arrested.

Patrolman Sherman Toler. Patrolman Toler was stationed in Tucumcari. He was commissioned on October 10, 1979. On March 5, 1986, he stopped a car on I-40 west of Tucumcari. The driver attacked him and took the officer's .357 service revolver and shot him five times, some rounds hitting his vest. The driver then beat Toler over the head with the pistol, killing him.

Patrolman/Pilot Wayne Allison. Patrolman Allison was stationed in Santa Fe. He was commissioned on November 27, 1985. On February 13, 1988, he had just taken off from Santa Fe in the state police aircraft to fly to Carlsbad. About 15 minutes into the flight, the plane flew straight into the ground. The National Transportation Safety Board ruled the cause of the crash to be undetermined.

PATROLMAN GLEN HUBER. Patrolman Huber, a member of the Tactical Team, was stationed in Espanola. He was commissioned on October 31, 1981. On January 26, 1991, he was shot and killed by a sniper. Earlier that day, a Rio Arriba County deputy arrived at a location to serve a restraining order. He did not find the subject at home. After he left, the suspect came home and shot and killed his girlfriend, his girlfriend's daughter, and the daughter's five-month-old son. He also killed the daughter's boyfriend and then killed his girlfriend's sister. Next, he shot and wounded a 13-year-old boy. The deputy sheriff soon drove back to the residence, where he was surprised and disarmed. He was then executed by the suspect. The state police began getting calls on shots fired. Patrolman Huber responded to the scene and stopped well back from the residence to look the situation over. He was shot and killed by the suspect with a scoped 7 mm rifle at 200 yards. The suspect escaped and later turned himself in.

Maj. Eugene Archibeque. Major Archibeque was stationed at headquarters in Santa Fe. He was commissioned on December 30, 1977. On August 11, 1993, he was jogging during his lunch hour and had a heart attack. He passed away in a local hospital.

Patrolman Lloyd Aragon Sr. Patrolman Aragon was stationed in Grants. He was commissioned on January 1, 1994. On August 1, 2001, he was assisting in a pursuit on I-40 east of Grants. He put a spike belt on the highway and then went into the median. The driver of the pursued vehicle intentionally drove into the median, striking Aragon and killing him instantly.

Patrolman Ramon Solis and Patrolman Damon Talbott. Patrolman Solis (right) and Patrolman Talbott (below) were stationed in Roswell and were members of Recruit School No. 64, which graduated on December 8, 2000. On October 19, 2001, they were killed while attending training involving a civilian medical helicopter. The patrolmen and another classmate, Jennifer Schurman, were riding in the hospital aircraft in order to learn procedures on how to set up landing zones at accident scenes. The pilot lost control and crashed, killing both patrolmen and injuring Schurman and the civilian pilot.

PATROLMAN JAMES ARCHULETA. Patrolman Archuleta was stationed in Espanola. He was commissioned on June 18, 2004. On June 4, 2006, he was killed in an automobile accident while responding to a call. Patrolman Archuleta was driving at night on US 84, north of Espanola, when he rounded a curve and struck a cow that was in the roadway. The unit then rolled over, ejecting Archuleta.

PATROLMAN CHRISTOPHER MIRABAL. Patrolman Mirabal was stationed in Alamogordo. He was commissioned on December 11, 1998, and was a member of the department's motor unit. On June 13, 2007, while attempting to stop a car in Alamogordo, Mirabal lost control and struck a curb. The motorcycle then hit a parked semitrailer, causing fatal injuries to the officer.

Lt. Michael Avilucea. Lieutenant Avilucea was stationed in Alamogordo and was the commander of the bomb team. He was commissioned on October 31, 1981. On May 30, 2008, Avilucea was driving southbound on US 84, south of Tierra Amarilla, returning from an Explosive Ordnance Disposal callout. For an unknown reason, he lost control of his department pickup and it rolled over, killing him.

Sgt./Pilot Andrew "Andy" Tingwall. Sergeant Tingwall was stationed in Santa Fe and was commissioned on December 1, 1995. On June 11, 2009, Tingwall died in a helicopter crash after he picked up a lost hiker on a mountain. There was severe weather when the helicopter crashed into the side of the mountain. Due to bad weather, the crash site was not reached until two days later.